TAYLOR
MADE

TAYLOR
MADE

A YEAR IN THE LIFE OF
AUSTRALIA'S CRICKET CAPTAIN

MARK TAYLOR

Foreword by Ian Chappell

First published 1995 in Macmillan by Pan Macmillan Australia Pty Limited
St Martins Tower, 31 Market Street, Sydney

National Library of Australia
cataloguing-in-publication data:

Taylor, Mark, 1964-
Taylor made
ISBN 0 7329 0822 1.
1. Taylor, Mark, 1964- . 2. Cricket captains -
Australia - Biography. I. Title
796.258092

Designed by Liz Seymour
Typeset in 10.5/14pt New Baskerville
Printed in Australia by Australian Print Group

Cricket has given me many opportunities, such as representing my country, touring various parts of the world and writing books such as Taylor Made.

It is a lifestyle I enjoy and would not exchange.

However, it does call for certain sacrifices, the greatest being giving up precious time with my wife, Judi, and my two sons, William (3) and Jack (6 months).

I would therefore like to dedicate this book to my family, whom I feel make the greatest sacrifice of all.

I'd also like to mention my extended family. My family in Sydney and my wife's family at Half-Way Creek in northern New South Wales both play a very important part in my life and, therefore, in this book.

MARK TAYLOR
Sydney, August 1995

Foreword

BY IAN CHAPPELL

'As well as making a century, I'd like you to win the toss.' That was the way New South Wales' selector Neil Marks broke the news to Mark Taylor — that he would captain the side for the first time in the Shield final of 1989-90.

Taylor barely had time to change into his creams before winning the toss as stand-in captain for the injured Geoff Lawson. He then proceeded to methodically dismantle the Queensland attack, made a century in each innings and led New South Wales to a comprehensive victory by 345 runs.

More than likely it was Mark's calm leadership at such short notice in this match that earmarked him as a future Australian captain. His outstanding performance could easily have convinced the hierarchy that he was the ideal man to handle a tough assignment — and that's exactly what he inherited when Allan Border eventually retired.

Not only was Taylor chosen to take over from a man who'd become a national hero after almost a decade on the job, but he was also expected to take his team on two demanding tours and in the process be pitted against Australia's toughest rivals in world cricket.

Undaunted, Taylor began by leading his men in an exciting series, which resulted in an excruciatingly narrow loss in Pakistan. They then returned home to thrash England and finally trooped off to the Caribbean and decisively beat the world champions, West Indies.

Following a marvellously mature performance in his first season as captain, Taylor has now convinced the rest of the country as well as the Australian Cricket Board that he's the right man for the job.

However, it's not just the spectacular results that Mark Taylor has achieved that have won him respect as Australian captain, but also the aggressive manner in which the team has sought victory. As a captain Taylor quickly recognised his team's assets and set about fully utilising them.

On his opening day as a Test captain against Pakistan in Karachi, Australia batted first and comfortably passed 300 by stumps. The pattern of aggressive strokeplay was established that day and has been assiduously maintained ever since, under Taylor's guiding hand. It has resulted in Australia being in a position to win most of the Tests under his leadership and this policy of subjecting the opposition to an all-out onslaught has quickly endeared him to the Australian cricket public.

The players who have benefited most from Taylor allowing the batsmen the freedom to express themselves have been Michael Slater, Mark Waugh and Greg Blewett. In return, Taylor is already benefiting from their exciting strokeplay by regularly chalking up wins as Australia's captain.

At a time when Test cricket needs as much assistance as possible, Mark Taylor shapes up as the man to set the example for other captains in making the game more entertaining. In addition, Taylor has shown himself to be tactically adept by using his bowlers wisely and placing his many talented fieldsmen in positions where they are likely to profit from the bowlers' accuracy. While watching the West Indies bat in the Caribbean there was hardly a moment when I didn't feel that a wicket was just around the corner. This makes the cricket interesting for the players as well as the spectators, something that should always be a high priority for a captain.

Mark's undemonstrative style as leader has been well-accepted by his men and they've shown themselves to be a side capable of handling the odd reversal and then hitting back hard. That is the sign of a good team.

Despite the West Indies' dominance in the One Day Internationals, Taylor's team identified some frailties in their opponents. Duly noted, this knowledge was then used to undermine the Windies as Australia gradually asserted their authority in the Test series. Taylor showed he has a good grasp of the psychological side of the game by using this hard-won intelligence to boost his team's spirit at the appropriate time and, in doing so, made Australia a more formidable opponent in enemy territory.

The team performed exceedingly well in Pakistan and the Caribbean — the first time in a long while that an Australian side has played to their potential away from home (apart from the two most recent tours of England). Under Taylor the Australian team dropped the siege mentality approach and the change worked wonders in Pakistan. It was there that Taylor won respect as a captain and this resulted in the team maintaining confidence in their ability to win in the Caribbean despite the disappointing loss in the One Day series.

This cool, calculated approach from Mark Taylor the captain is no surprise. From the moment he batted serenely in his first Test against a fearsome West Indies pace attack, it was obvious that temperament was a strong point in his game. It helps him enormously as skipper, as he's not easily flustered or panicked into doing something rash. These qualities were in evidence when he took over from an injured Border a couple of times in One Day matches and performed with credit not only as a captain, but also as a player.

Most of all it has been the exciting style the Australian team has adopted in going about their job under Mark Taylor which has impressed.

As a commentator on the game I believe it's important to be impartial, but that doesn't mean in any way that I can't appreciate the Australian team playing good cricket. I have admired Mark Taylor's captaincy which is tailor-made for the modern game in which a team not only has to win, but also entertain, to satisfy the patrons.

IAN CHAPPELL
JUNE 1995

Mark Taylor, Ian Chappell and the Frank Worrell trophy.

CONTENTS

Introduction

BY IAN HEADS

Mark Taylor had something extra tucked into the 'coffin' that carted his cricket gear over thousands of kilometres through the first helter-skelter year of his tenure as Australian captain. A small tape recorder travelled almost as widely as Mark did, and was his constant companion through the thrilling months of the West Indies campaign which provided the climax to the year. In the quiet of his room after a hectic day of cut and thrust in the centre, Australia's 39th captain would record his innermost thoughts. This book, *Taylor Made*, releasing for the first time that intensely private material, is the product of Mark's endeavours, capturing uniquely what it is to be Australia's cricket captain — 'the second most important man in Australia' as Channel Nine's Ray Martin put it to Mark in an early interview, May 1994.

Bluff, straightforward Mark Taylor never saw himself that way. He's very much a man of the people, an ordinary bloke who just happens to be a tough and outstanding cricketer with a wonderful feel for the ancient game. Succeeding his friend Allan Border — the admired 'AB' from whom he learned what it was to be tough on a cricket field — Taylor quickly went about putting his own stamp on the job. That stamp — of positive aggression, of taking the fight to his team's opponents, whoever they happened to be — produced a year of wonderful cricket, and striking success.

The Aussies under Taylor were beaten by a whisker in a magnificent and controversial series in Pakistan and then comprehensively despatched the oldest enemy, England, in the Australian summer. After a one-day triumph in New Zealand came the crowning glory, a breathtaking win against the world champion West Indians in the Caribbean. This last, memorable achievement was testimony to both the fighting qualities of the current Australian team under Taylor and to the personal strength of the man who is now their leader. Even in the darkest hours — a clear beating in the one-dayers, a disastrous day in Trinidad when the third Test slipped away, skipper Taylor was never 'down', never beaten. There were times he had every right to be. For a visiting team in the West Indies to lose *both* key strike bowlers with injury (Craig McDermott and Damien Fleming) as the Australian team did was surely a pathway to disaster and certain defeat. These indomitable Aussies under Taylor, merely shrugged and got on with business — leaving the best to last with the sensational win in Jamaica that wrapped up the series, and plunged West Indian cricket into mourning.

Taylor Made provides many insights into Australia's captain and into the men around him — the Waughs, David Boon, Shane Warne and the rest — and into the highs and lows of touring and playing the game of cricket at its supreme level. But more than anything else it reveals why Mark Taylor *is* Australia's captain and is likely to be for the long haul. His positive approach — making attack the best form of defence at all times — is a breakthrough from conservatism and refreshing indeed for both Australian and world cricket. According to Taylor, cricket matches are there to be won via an intelligent, aggressive and always-positive approach — no matter what names happen to be on the team sheet in the other dressing-room.

So join Mark Taylor on a personal odyssey which began with his being 'smuggled' to Sydney in May '94 (so there would be no giveaway to who Australia's next captain was to be) and ended in the sunshine of beautiful Bermuda as the Australians played the dreamy social matches which came at the end of the West Indies campaign — bathing all the while in the glow of what they had so recently achieved against the fearsome Windies. Taylor-made indeed! . . . that's Australia's new captain.

IAN HEADS
JULY 1995

CLIMBING THE MOUNTAIN

Chapter 1

THE LONG MARCH

It all began a long time ago, on summer-baked malthoid pitches in the town of my boyhood years, Wagga. I have been a cricketer since the year 1973 and the familiar path along which I have trekked in all the seasons since, through juniors, grade, Sheffield Shield and then beyond, is worn with the imprint of many boots. But to arrive at the point I did on May 19, 1994 — to be whisked to Sydney in a cloak-and-dagger operation and announced as Australia's new captain — is something that still stretches my own belief. In the pages that follow, after a brief preamble on the earlier life and times of M. Taylor cricketer, I reflect on the good times and bad of the most extraordinary year of my life, as Test skipper in a crowded, hectic and ultimately wonderful twelve months.

My first-class career began on 25 October, 1985, when I was selected from my club side Northern District to represent New South Wales. I made my debut for the State against Tasmania at Hobart's TCA Ground, although I must be honest and admit that the only reason I got the call for the Blues was because our incumbent openers Steve Smith and John Dyson had been banned from State cricket after taking part in the upcoming rebel tour of South Africa. Nor was I the only beneficiary of the pair's omission. Mark Waugh was another youngster promoted with me to fill the gap. I made 12 and a pretty ordinary – and lucky – 56 not out in that first outing, but things got better for me and I went on to have a reasonable first season as a State opener. We won the Sheffield Shield that year.

Without setting the game alight, I enjoyed another sound season for NSW in 1986-87 and soon after there was talk in cricket's inner circles that I might get the call to play for Australia.

During that 1986-87 season the Australian side lost the first and fourth Tests to England in the Ashes series. The fifth Test was to be played at the SCG and on the morning the team was to be announced I received a phone call from a woman at Channel Nine, informing me that I had been selected in the team. The call came at 6 a.m. and she asked me if I would drive to the channel's Artarmon (Sydney) studios to appear on the *Today* program. I accepted gladly, and jumped in the shower. Twenty minutes later the phone rang again — the same woman, this time to ask me if there was a "P. Taylor" who played cricket for NSW. I told her her, there certainly was — Peter Taylor — and there was a pregnant pause. Then she told me that on her team sheet the name of the new player in was P. Taylor. Could that be Peter and not me who had made the side, she asked. It could well be, I said. At that point I declined the invitation to appear on the program.

At 9.15 that morning I took a phone call from New South Wales captain Dirk Wellham who had been named in the Test side. It was Dirk who relayed the news beyond doubt that it was Peter, and not me, who had been called up. At least for three hours I had experienced the feeling of being selected for Australia's Test team. But deep down, despite the mix-up and the disappointment of that morning, I knew I wasn't quite ready.

By 1989 it was a different matter. With the West Indies touring Australia, I made 83 for New South Wales against a good Western Australian side whose attack boasted Bruce Reid and Terry Alderman and as a result was picked to appear for Australia in the fourth Test, to begin on Australia Day, January 26, 1989, at the Sydney Cricket Ground. We were down 3-0 in the series at that stage and in dire straits, but I remember when I joined the side I felt good. There was a *very* good feeling all round. In spite of the fact that we were copping a hiding at the hands of the Windies, my team-mates were jovial, too. There weren't too many blokes with their heads down. I credit that to our skipper Allan Border.

Things took a turn for the better in that fourth Test. The West Indies batted first and we dismissed them for 224, with AB taking 7/46. Being in the field gave me a chance to soak up the tense atmosphere of a Test before having to face the Windies' fast bowling barrage of Ambrose, Marshall and Walsh. But of course my moment of truth arrived. My first Test run came when a Curtly Ambrose ripper deflected off my thigh guard. I took off and as I completed the run I gestured to the umpire that I had hit the ball with my bat, so he wouldn't call a leg bye. Somehow my charade was convincing, and I was off the mark. When I was on 5, Curtly yorked me. It was a great delivery. I looked around and my stumps were everywhere. I was walking when I heard the umpire call 'No-ball!' Curtly was kicking the dirt in rage.

No-ball or not, Curtly Ambrose had beaten me badly, and my confidence for a time was in as much disarray as my stumps had been. But after my reprieve I progressed steadily to 25 and was beginning to think maybe, just maybe, I was good enough to match it with the world's best. Then, just when I looked like settling in for a reasonable score, Ambrose had his revenge. Another yorker, same result — stumps everywhere. This time the umpire didn't intervene and I was history. As I trudged off I thought, 'Hey, I'm going to play at least one Test match — which is one more than I probably deserve to play.' In the second innings I made 3, caught in the gully off Ambrose. We won the match by seven wickets, with Allan Border grabbing a bag of 11 wickets with his left arm slows. In the fifth Test in Adelaide I notched 3 and 36 before being run out in both innings. With a total of 67 runs in four digs, I believed my chances of selection in the Australian squad for the 1989 tour of England had to be remote. No way was I good enough.

The selectors thought otherwise. I made the team for England where I scored 839 runs in six Test matches, a performance bettered only by Donald Bradman in Australian cricket history. We left Australia that year rated by at least one newspaper as: 'The worst Australian side to leave our shores'. We returned months later heads held high, 4-0 winners of the Ashes series. And if rain had not intervened in the third and sixth Tests we would have won 6-0. As it was the 4-0 result matched the Ashes record set by Bradman's team in 1948.

I believe this series represented the turning point for Australian Test cricket. We had won the World Cup for the one-day game, but our Test record over the previous 8-10 years had been ordinary. In this series, we learned how to win. Steve Waugh and I both had good series with the bat, Ian Healy his best so far with the gloves. All of a sudden along with the experienced core of Allan Border, David Boon and Geoff Marsh we had the wider nucleus of a competitive, settled side. I saw the ball so well all that English summer. It reached the stage where I just didn't believe the Pommie bowlers could get me out. Talk about a turnaround! The run avalanche continued the following summer against Pakistan when I scored heavily against Waqar Younis, Wasim Akram, Aaqib Javed and Mushtaq Ahmed. At the end of that series Deloittes Rating System, which rates the world's best bowlers and batsmen against one another, pegged me as Best Batsman in the World.

At the end of the 1991-92 season Lawrie Sawle, the Australian chairman of selectors, rang me at home. He told me I had been named AB's vice-captain for the upcoming tour of Sri Lanka in August. I was elated, knowing that this appointment was a signal from the powers-that-be that I was in line one day to captain Australia. Then, when my elation calmed down, I felt sorry for the man I had replaced as vice-captain, Geoff Marsh — 'Swampy', as we called him, my fellow opener and a friend. A couple of days after Sawle's phone call to me, I made one of my own. I rang Swampy in Perth to see how he was going in the light of the announcement. His wife, Michelle, a lovely lady, answered the phone and said to me, 'Oh, congratulations, but you've got my husband's job!' She was right: I did, and I really felt that I had stolen it from him. You don't like to do things like that, especially when Marsh's losing the vice-captaincy was a sign that his days of playing for his country were over too. Someone wins, someone loses.

The next major milestone in my career, I'm sorry to say, was getting dropped. I'd had a good series against the Windies in the Caribbean in 1991, averaging 49. In Sri Lanka in August '92 I'd had a good one-day series but didn't perform up to expectations in the Tests, finishing with an average of only 25. Still, when the West Indies toured here in 1992-93 I was champing at the bit, convinced it was going to be a big year for me, especially when I hit a hundred against them for New South Wales early in the tour. But my confidence in myself was misplaced. By the deciding fifth Test in Perth I was twelfth man after a string of ordinary scores, and I knew I deserved to carry the drinks. That hurt. I'd played poorly all summer. God bless the selectors, though, because they reinstated me as opener and vice-captain for our three-Test tour of New Zealand in early 1993. I got amongst the runs and my career was back on track.

I have mixed memories of our tour of South Africa in 1994. It was a disappointing series from both a team and an individual point of view. It turned out to be AB's swansong, and we wanted to do well for him as well as ourselves, but things didn't work out as we'd have wished. Part of the problem was that we went to South Africa just wanting to play cricket, without really considering the political implications of taking part in South Africa's re-emergence into international cricket. We saw the trip as three Tests, eight one-dayers, just part of our cricket caravan, just another few weeks on the road. It turned out to be much more than this, with the eyes of the cricketing world charting our progress on this history-making tour.

We were badly upset when, after Shane Warne and Merv Hughes got into strife for sledging in the first Test, they were made examples of by our own Cricket Board and fined $4 000 each after the ICC match referee, Donald Carr, had given them only a slap on the wrist (a $400 fine) for their transgressions. In hindsight we should have known that we had to be on our best behaviour. Before the series Alan Crompton, chairman of the ACB, had said publicly that he wanted to stamp sledging out of the game, that abusing opponents was un-Australian and unmanly. Shane Warne was fined for directing verbal abuse (i.e. sledging) at Andrew Hudson after dismissing him in the second innings. Merv was fined for repeated verbal abuse of the South African batsmen during the game. Neither incident was a major one. But in the light of Alan Crompton's pre-match remarks they took on much wider significance.

My view of sledging is this — I don't believe it works. I can't think of any player who has been put off his game by verbal abuse. However, in any serious sporting contest — and international cricket is certainly that — there is always going to be the odd word said in the heat of battle. I do not see any problem with that, as long as it is kept reasonably in check and not allowed, by the player or his captain, to extend past the brief moment when it happens. Of course, without excusing their behaviour, the furore was blown right up by the media, with repeated replays of both incidents. Even when I returned home, everyone was asking me, 'What did Warnie say to Andrew Hudson when he got him out? What did Merv say?' and so on.

The controversy didn't help our mental preparedness for what turned into a tough series against a South African side with plenty to prove to the world that had excluded them for so long. When we arrived there it was one Test all, after the Australian leg of the series. The South Africans won in Johannesburg, and we beat them in Cape Town, so it was two Tests apiece when we met for the decider in Durban. The game turned into an absolute nightmare for us. They sent us in to bat on a wicket that was doing a bit. We made 269. They answered with 422, accumulated painfully slowly over 200 overs. That left them a whole day and a session to bowl us out on what had become by that stage a good wicket. It could have been one of the great Test matches, but it ended in one of the most boring draws I have ever played in. By batting for so long in their first innings to accumulate 422 the South Africans left us with no option but to play out time and hope for a draw. They did their best to bowl us out, but the match was set to peter out from a long, long way before stumps on the final day. As the last Test of the series and, as it turned out, AB's last-ever Test, it was a disappointing event — unsatisfactory for everyone, players and spectators alike.

I learned plenty being vice-captain to Allan. He was thrown into the hot seat in the mid-80s when things weren't going well for the national side, and from what I understand, from himself and others, he was a reluctant skipper at first.

All he really wanted to do was play, to compete. He was the fiercest competitor I've known. He lived for cricket. He would always be one of the last to leave the dressing room, lingering to have a few beers and chat — to anyone — about the game he loved. I always thought he'd get sick of cricket, playing it, talking about it, but he never did. From AB I learned to be tough on the field. I also learned the value of talking cricket with him and other greats of the past like Bob Simpson and Ian Chappell. These men had so much to teach a young bloke. You never knew when they were about to come out with a gem that would shed light on cricket and captaincy.

Another fine skipper who helped me no end was my Northern District club skipper Ross Turner, who now works for the New South Wales Cricket Association. Captain of the side in the two years when we won the Sydney first-grade comp, Ross was someone I looked up to. He was a great communicator, and I don't think I ever heard him raise his voice. He just got the job done. He was able to talk to — and get through to — all different kinds of people. He knew how to extract from his men the very best they were capable of giving. As a student of human nature, Ross knew the guys he had to roast and the ones who responded best after being buttered up. Our Northern District side was not the most talented in the competition, but our opponents knew that every time we took the field we would play to the best of our potential, thanks to Ross's inspiring captaincy. If our opposition didn't play to the best of theirs, they'd lose.

Border was not a communicator like Turner. He was a little more distant, and just got on with the job with no fuss or frills. For a start, AB was eight or so years older than the rest of us in the Australian side. We looked up to him and would follow him anywhere. Where Ross Turner cajoled us, AB led by example. Right or wrong, our respect for him was so great we did whatever he told us. He grew up in an era when what the senior players said went. Younger men were not encouraged to contribute. These days it's different, at least in the Aussie side. As skipper, I want to hear from everyone. Ian Healy, David Boon, Steve Waugh, Craig McDermott and the others have so much knowledge I'd be mad not to listen to them. Obviously as captain I'm in charge, but I think guys play better when they feel valued so I encourage my men to put in their two bob's worth.

I was disappointed by the way Allan's retirement came about. After captaining Australia for ten years and being a Test regular for fifteen, AB was a legend. That last year, when he was thirty-nine, there was intense speculation on the exact timing of what most people thought was his imminent decision to call it quits. Around April 1994, nearing the end of our tour of South Africa, I buttonholed him at a function and said, 'Look, I don't know if you are going to retire or not but if you do, congratulations on your career and I've really enjoyed playing under you.' I meant those words, I really did. Playing under AB was a great part of my life. He looked at me and said, 'Tubs, between you, me and the gatepost, this is my last tour. I will be calling it quits. But you know me, I don't like all the hullabaloo that goes with retirement. All the press and the big song-and-dance tributes. I'm going to wait a month and then I'll officially retire when the football season is on and no-one's even thinking about cricket.' That to me summed up AB. He hated all the hoopla — all he wanted to do was play the game at the highest level he was capable of. He was a man who could happily live without the public adulation, the press conferences and the autograph hunters who dogged him.

In early May 1994 Ian Healy, David Boon, Steve Waugh and I were summoned to a meeting in the Australian Cricket Board offices in Melbourne. We were informed that AB would be making an announcement regarding his cricket future within a week. The ACB added that we should understand that we were only being given advance notice because we were the side's senior players; it was not a meeting to discuss who would succeed Allan as skipper. They pointed out that Allan was still captain of Australia and would remain so for as long as he wanted the job. We agreed with that. AB was the man in charge, we were devoted to him, and he could keep the position as long as he damn-well pleased. We felt at the time that, still being the man in charge, AB should have been at that meeting too, especially when we were asked questions on team form, morale and so on. I believe that when AB heard of the meeting he was upset. He assumed it was a meeting to sound out possible future captains and was angry because he believed we were holding discussions about his team behind his back. That certainly wasn't so.

There was no retirement announcement from Allan that week. Then suddenly in the middle of the week after that came the news that the Australian Test captain had officially announced his retirement — not at cricket headquarters at the ACB offices in Melbourne, but on a Queensland golf course, giving his mate Pat Welsh and Channel Seven the exclusive story. I felt that at the time of his retirement AB was upset with the Board. There was a bitter edge to his interview with Pat Welsh. For a great Australian sportsman to depart feeling that way, from a game he loved and which he had served for so long, was a matter of disappointment to cricket fans everywhere. Allan's choice was for a quiet retirement — but for a man of his high profile and status that was never going to be easy. I am unsure of where the ultimate blame lies — whether with the Board, the senior players or Allan himself . . . or whether it was a combination of all three — but I'm sure that everyone in the game of cricket was saddened to see such an illustrious career reach an ending that was so unsatisfactory. It's a shame we can't have an instant replay for a man who had made such a wonderful contribution. The great thing is, of course, that Allan Border will not be remembered for the way he retired — but for the momentous nature of his career.

With AB gone, the ACB's top priority was to appoint his successor. I believe there were four serious candidates: Ian Healy, Steve Waugh, David Boon and me, with Heals and yours truly, as the incumbent vice-captain, the favourites. There was all kinds of speculation at the time, from inside cricketing circles and in the press. They were saying a New South Welshman shouldn't be picked because New South Wales already had too much power. They were saying Heals had to be overlooked because wicketkeeper is not the ideal position from which to skipper a side. So Ian and I got together and made a vow. We both wanted the job badly, we both knew that, but I told him if he got the nod ahead of me I'd support him all the way, and he said the same to me. Whatever happened, we agreed, we'd both get on and do what we did best: play cricket.

I think, looking back, that all four of us had serious claims to the leadership. Heals had been a regular member of the Test and one-day teams since 1988. He was — and is — an inspirational fellow and a real patriot. He has become a superb keeper and is a dependable batsman who can keep his wicket when others are panicking and losing theirs. Boonie has been an out-and-out champion for years. Brave and a true world-class batsman, his only negative was his age. He was thirty-two then and this could have gone against him. A lot of people are loath to select a captain who will only be around a couple more years. 'Tugger' Waugh would have been an excellent choice because he has an astute cricketing brain, is aggressive and is a real competitor. His lack of captaincy experience may have told against him.

I was AB's deputy, so I had to be in the box seat. My Test position as an opening batsman was secure, but on the downside, my tenure in the Australian one-day team was not nearly so safe. In fact, I had been in and out of the one-day side all season. Some said I lacked the fitness and mobility for one-day contests, others that I just wasn't too good at the game. It's history now that I was named Australian captain for Tests and one-day Internationals. My form in both has been good ever since, so hopefully I'm making some of my old critics eat their words.

Chapter 2

CLOAK
AND DAGGER
CAPTAINCY

'Tubbie, you're it.' It was Ian McDonald calling on his mobile to my friend and former Northern District and Test team-mate Peter Taylor's farm at Gurley, thirty kilometres south of Moree. I was holing up at Peter's waiting to learn if I'd be the next Australian captain. Macca had returned to Sydney from the ACB meeting in Melbourne that afternoon where it was decided I should take over as skipper. He went on, 'Yes, Mark, you're it. You're the next captain. There's a press conference at midday tomorrow so be on the eight o'clock flight to Sydney tomorrow morning. We've already booked your ticket. Your vice-captain is Ian Healy.' Macca's next three calls were to Heals, Steve Waugh and David Boon to let them know the news.

I think Peter Taylor was more excited at the news than I was. Of course, I felt great pride at being named the thirty-ninth Australian captain, but I could foresee the work and responsibility that were in store for me. My wife Judi was happy for me too, but she also had that look in her eye that told me we were going to have to endure some tough times in the months and years ahead. I would be spending less time with her, less time with my son William. There would be intense media pressure. The way I led the team, the way I played, the decisions I made, would all be mercilessly scrutinised and analysed. No wonder I was a little subdued. Proud, yes, but a little in awe of the testing times that lay ahead. Peter, however, was ecstatic for me and on for a party. He produced two bottles of champagne from his fridge and popped the cork of one. But after drinking two glasses with him I announced, 'I'm going to bed.' I'm sure I disappointed Peter, who was keen to get stuck into the second bottle and even go to the pub to buy more if need be. But I cried off his hospitality. I was mentally tired after the long days of waiting and uncertainty. I knew I had a big day coming up and I wanted to be fresh for the press conference.

That day, May 19, 1994, turned out to be one of the greatest — but at the same time one of the funniest — days of my life. I got out of bed at Peter's at 6 a.m., showered and climbed into my best dark green suit, which I'd taken to the bush with me in anticipation of being summoned back to Sydney to meet the press. So there I was in the back of nowhere, dressed to the nines, when Peter insisted on giving me a lift to the airport at Moree in his 1971 diesel-powered semi-trailer. The damn thing had metal seats covered in grime and grease. There was grease everywhere. I told him I would drive myself but he wouldn't hear of it. 'I've got to go past the airport anyway to pick up some farm equipment,' he said, wiping grease from the cabin with a rag, 'so I'll take you.' When we got to the airport, we had to park out in the street because the semi-trailer was too big to fit into the parking area.

Then came our next problem. Ian McDonald, determined that no news of my appointment got out before the official announcement at the press conference, had taken the precaution of booking my ticket in the name of Peter Taylor, lest an airline employee see that Mark Taylor was catching an early flight to Sydney and put two and two together and ring the media with a hot tip that

I'd been given the nod. That meant I had to convince the girl behind the desk that it was Mark and not Peter Taylor who had to catch that flight. That took time. Finally we sorted it all out and I sat down in the gate. There was one other person there. He was a farmer, obviously waiting to meet a passenger on the flight from Sydney. He recognised me at once and came over and sat down beside me. He was wearing overalls and had a western shirt on underneath and knew his cricket. He said, 'Now let me . . . I think you're Mark Taylor.'

I said, 'Yeah, you're right, mate.'

He continued, 'G'day . . . Now you're going back to Sydney on the eight o'clock flight?'

'That's correct,' I said.

He said, 'Now, Allan Border retired last week, didn't he? And you're the vice-captain. I reckon you're off to Sydney because you're the next captain.'

So I said, 'Mate, if you can work all that out, you've got a four-hour exclusive because no-one else in Australia is going to find that out till midday.' So some Moree farmer was the first member of the general public to know I was the new Australian captain. I reckon he'll have a story to tell his mates in the pub for the rest of his life.

Arriving in Sydney I was met by Ian McDonald, who drove me straight to the New South Wales Cricket Association offices in Druitt Street. There I was hustled into a back room while the media assembled in the conference rooms for the big news. At midday McDonald, Alan Crompton, Chairman of the ACB, and Graham Halbish, Chief Executive Officer, fronted the press who were there in droves with their cameras, microphones and notepads and told them that Mark Taylor was the thirty-ninth Australian cricket captain. At that cue to make my entrance, I walked into the room to answer questions. It was then that the enormity of the job I had taken on sank in. The room was crammed full of people hanging on my words, not just sporting scribes either. There was a live television cross to Derryn Hinch on the *Midday Show.*

I was completely unprepared for the barrage of questions. I really thought the press conference would be purely a backslapping exercise with everyone congratulating me and me just saying, 'Blah, blah, blah, she'll be right.' Not so. The mood in the room was good and I was aware that everyone wished me well, but the press guys hit me with some hard questions and came at me thick and fast. What was my ambition for the team? Would I be an aggressive captain? How would coach Bob Simpson and I share the workload? What was my attitude to sledging? As I said, I had no answers prepared, but I spoke honestly. On sledging, I said that I thought that we Australians did not sledge as often as many people thought. Our so-called sledging had been overplayed, not least by the press, for some years. Maybe we were wearing the wrap for indiscretions of past teams of the '70s and '80s when we had a reputation for abusing opponents, giving umpires a hard time and pushing every rule to its limit. Now, I said, we were not a soft side. We played tough cricket and always would. So, said the media, what happened in South Africa when Merv Hughes and Shane Warne were fined for sledging opponents? Good point. But I pointed out what I believed to be the case. Any time we'd lost it on the field and unleashed verbal abuse at opponents had been when we'd been playing badly, when we'd got frustrated, when things had gone against us and we hadn't taken our chances. For short periods of time, like in South Africa, we'd lost the plot. Lately though, we'd been realising why we had vented frustration on opposing batsmen and bowlers and had moved to short-circuit the aggro, get our minds back on cricket and turn our fortunes around. It was all about self-control.

I added, too, that international cricket these days was a tough job, hard work. We played now for nine months of the year and for four or five of those we were overseas, away from loved ones and friends and our normal lifestyle. Sometimes places we played weren't as nice as Australia, and accommodation could be substandard, the crowds against us. But we had to understand that all this had to be taken in our stride and that we had to go out every day and play hard, fair cricket. In my time in the national side, that was mostly what we'd done. There had been the odd occasion when we'd behaved badly, but these were rare and getting rarer. Unfortunately, some of the press used those times as their yardstick and painted us as the Ugly Australians.

I was pretty comfortable in my talk with the press that day. I guess I had never seen the media as the 'monsters' which seems to be the perception of some sportsmen. To me, that day and before and since, they are just people I have got to know over my nine years in first-class cricket. I have shared a drink and a joke with many of them, and in the main I respect the job they do. There have certainly been occasions when I've had bad press. The fact is that batsmen 'fail' at times. The media to me are no more than a bunch of people trying to do a job. Their job is to accurately report the events of the game. My job as captain is to provide as much information as I can to help the press to relate accurate reports on the day's events. If it happens that I do my job correctly, but they report inaccurately, then problems can arise. So far during my time as captain there haven't been any major problems and I can only hope that situation continues.

After the press conference, I jumped into a limo provided by Channel Nine and, sipping champagne, headed across the Harbour Bridge to their studios at Willoughby where I was to tape an interview with Ray Martin for *A Current Affair* that night. Sharing the back seat with me was *Sports Sunday* reporter Michael Meagher who, with the cameras rolling, fired questions at me. At Channel Nine I sat down opposite Ray Martin and the interview began.

'The first question I want to throw at you, Mark, is how do you feel taking over the second most important job in Australia, next only to the Prime Minister?' I had to tell him that he was wrong, that while Australians love their sport and especially their cricket, I didn't see being captain of the Aussie team as carrying anywhere near the same responsibility as that shouldered by, say, a politician. If I did a bad job, the worst that could happen was that we'd lose a Test. But if a politician stuffed up he could destroy the nation's economy and plunge the whole country into hardship. I would never want to be a politician. But Ray kept on assuring me that cricket captain was the second top job in Australia. Finally I told him I was in cricket to enjoy it and as soon as I stopped enjoying the game or started captaining badly I would quit. Ray asked me about nine more questions, then I did an interview for *Sports Sunday* and after that it was back into the limo and off to the Sydney Cricket Ground for a photo session.

At about 4.30 p.m. my media commitments were done so it was a relief to repair to the Lord Nelson Hotel in Paddington for a few quiet, relaxing glasses of champagne with Ian McDonald, Alan Crompton and Graham Halbish. No press, no clamour, just us. Before I left the pub I persuaded Crompton to buy me two bottles of Veuve Clicquot champagne to take back to Moree with me on the 6 p.m. flight to share with Peter Taylor, his family and my wife Judi. I didn't think there was any way they'd have French champagne in Moree. Waiting at Moree were Peter, his wife Julie and their daughter Sally Marie plus Judi and our son William who had stayed at the farm while I made my trek to Sydney. The Taylors whisked us off to a very nice restaurant called Cascades. The manager came over and congratulated me. I produced the two bottles of champagne and said, 'Can we have these opened, please?' The manager looked at them and said, 'You didn't need to bring these, we have Veuve Clicquot here, we got some in especially for your celebration. We knew you'd be feeling happy tonight.' We had a wonderful seafood meal and at the end the proprietor refused to let us pay for either the food or the champagne. I protested, but he insisted and I thanked him dearly. It was a terrific night to finish off a memorable day.

Next morning we packed the car and drove to Glen Innes where my wife's cousin and family live. We planned to stay with them for a bit. We all met up at the Club Hotel in Glen Innes for a meal before heading out to their place about thirty kilometres out of town. In the pub I walked up to the bar to buy a round of drinks and the publican looked at me closely and said, 'Geez, you look like that Mark Taylor bloke who's just been named Australian cricket captain.'

I decided to have a little fun with him. 'You're kidding, aren't you?' I said.

'No, you look exactly like him,' said the publican.

I replied, 'Oh yeah, but I'm better looking than Mark Taylor.'

He looked at me doubtfully and said, 'Yeah, well I suppose you are.' He served me the drinks but kept looking hard at me as I took my seat at our table. When it was Rex Chard's (Judi's cousin) turn to buy a round the publican couldn't help himself.

'Gosh, that bloke you're sitting with looks like Mark Taylor,' he said to Rex.

Finally Rex replied, 'Look, mate, you're a bloody idiot. It *is* Mark Taylor.' The poor bloke came over straightaway and apologised for the confusion and

I've never seen anyone go so red with embarrassment. But I told him not to worry, he was just a victim of my practical joke. He got even, I suppose, when he made a call to a mate who worked on the local newspaper and he turned up in a few minutes with a photographer. I was forced to give him an interview at the pub and pose for pictures. My life, I knew immediately, was no longer my own. Here I was in Glen Innes, not exactly a city, and the first pub I go into I'm doing an interview with the guy from the local rag. The demands on my time have not decreased in the months since. Wherever I go, whatever I do, whether it's the cricket season or not, people are going to recognise me and want some of my time. It comes with the territory.

Chapter 3

LIVING
WITH THE JOB

I've tried at all times to be a relaxed captain of Australia. From day one I have made a conscious effort not to change too much from the man I was before the announcement on May 19, 1994. Having said that, there are some changes I've had to make. For instance, now I must make sure at all times that I set — and am *seen* to set — a good example as skipper. That runs the gamut from the way I carry myself on the field, the decisions I make and my batting and fielding, to giving it my all at training and at all times acting as a good role model in the street, club or pub. A captain has to make certain sacrifices, both on and off the field. Occasionally I have to distance myself from the guys in the team. It is not something I like doing, but it is important that I am aware of setting an example for the younger players to follow.

I do, however, try not to let cricket govern my whole life. Ever since I was a little boy growing up in the sports-mad town of Wagga, playing cricket, footy or whatever was going, cricket has never been the be-all and end-all to me. My private life is more important. I try to spend time away from the game when my schedule permits. On those odd days when I do get to spend time with my family and friends — who are all such a wonderful part of my life — the press finds me all but impossible to contact. I have two boys now, William and Jack, and I miss them terribly when I'm away on tour or meeting my press commitments.

Then there is the public. A few nuisances bother you, demand autographs and call out to you in the street without even stopping to consider that they're invading your privacy. I usually don't mind signing autographs, but when someone thrusts a piece of paper under your nose and says, 'Sign that!' I do object. Then there's the other extreme. Just a few days after the interview in the Glen Innes pub, I was in a supermarket in Grafton, just strolling around the aisles, when I became aware of a boy — he would have been about ten — following me carrying a pen and paper. He must have tagged along behind me for about twenty minutes. I realised he wanted an autograph, but felt he should learn to ask politely for one. As much as intrusive people bug me, I think it annoys me more when people shy away from me in awe just because I'm a cricketer, and see me as aloof and unapproachable. I wanted him to front me and ask for the autograph, but he wouldn't. Finally, I walked out into the street where the boy was waiting for me with his mother.

She said, 'Would you mind signing this for my son?'

I said to her, 'No problem. An autograph takes me five seconds to sign, but you should tell your little boy to come to me straight out and ask would I mind signing it for him.' I gave him the autograph and I hope he learned a valuable lesson — that whether you're an unknown or captain of Australia we're all human beings.

Another demand on my time is to work closely with the Australian Cricket Board. They want to know my views on everything about cricket: the players, their form, the opposition, marketing — the works. I want the Australian cricket team and the ACB to have better communication than they've had in the past. In previous years there has been an us-versus-them mentality. To an extent there will always be a division between the players and the administrators, but we can get a lot closer than we have been. I'm trying to get clear lines of communication going between the cricketers and the Board on such subjects as why we have to go on certain tours, our pay, and other vital Board decisions that affect the team. With enlightened men such as Crompton and Halbish on the board, I'm sure it won't be long till the air is cleared and the administrators are welcoming input from the players on issues that concern them. I'm happy to see the inroads we have made in a short time.

In August 1994, just a month before we were to leave for a tour of Sri Lanka and Pakistan, Bob Simpson and the ACB organised a training camp for the touring squad in Adelaide. The aim of the four-day get-together was to get us fit — physically and mentally — for the gruelling campaign ahead. The ACB nutritionist, Lorna Garden, talked to us about nutrition and diet and we had a sports psychologist, Graham Winter, who held a workshop on goal-setting, which some players find useful. Graham is an excellent guy and helped our state of mind a lot, but me, I've never needed psychologists in general. I've always been my own psychologist, able to set my own goals and try to meet them. Another visitor to the camp was Channel Nine's sports director, Gary Burns, who addressed us on his station's coverage of cricket and invited questions from the players on the role and responsibilities of commentators, how they viewed and highlighted certain incidents on the field. All good, healthy discussion, because many of the boys get annoyed when small events are blown out of proportion.

Finally, I used the time away together to establish myself as captain, tell the guys how I perceived my role, and establish what we expected from each other. I said that as skipper the final responsibility for all decisions was mine. Hopefully I would make correct decisions, but if I was wrong I would be the one to wear the flak. Most importantly, I told them I welcomed their input, advice and expertise at all times. Every member of that team had to know that my door would always be open to him. 'Communicate with me on and off the field and at team meetings and over a beer, whenever,' I said. 'Let me know how you're feeling about your bowling, batting or fielding. If I know how you're feeling it's easier for me to make decisions. Communication is the key to becoming a better team.'

Chapter 4

THE ONE
THAT GOT AWAY —
PAKISTAN '94

The response to my team talk in Adelaide had been so positive that at the start of our tour of Pakistan I called another meeting with the men who had real influence over the team: our strike bowlers Craig McDermott and Shane Warne, and batsmen David Boon, and Mark and Steve Waugh. I chatted to them again about what I expected from them. Throughout that tour I was glad we'd spent the time together laying the ground rules of our campaign. The spirit throughout was excellent in spite of quite a few things not going our way. We were whacked hard by injuries, with all seven bowlers being hurt at one stage. We lost the first Test in Karachi by a whisker and if the side wasn't to a man filled with good blokes things could have got nasty after that. It could have developed into one of those tours where everyone thinks, 'Oh no, another tour of the subcontinent, another nightmare.' But the guys really hung in there well and I ended up really enjoying the tour, my first as skipper. I thought, 'If I can keep this kind of feeling among the boys for the rest of my career, that'll do me.'

But while I was happy with the team, I can't say the same about my own early form with the bat. In the first game against a President's XI at Rawalpindi, the wicket had a little bit in it and I scored four runs in the first innings and one in the second. I wasn't hitting the ball at all well, and the press picked up on that. When you're on your first tour as captain the media contingent really put you under the microscope, especially when you're playing poorly. They kept asking me what was the matter and what was I going to do about it. I told them that the Tests had not started yet and that I would assess my form after the first Test in Karachi. Well, in that first Test, and my first as captain, I made a pair. My first innings as skipper, two noughts. The wicket was an absolute belter, very flat, with nothing in it for the bowlers. But when I went to turn a ball from Wasim Akram to the leg side in my first innings I hit the ball straight back to him for a simple caught and bowled. Not the start I wanted, by any means. Thank goodness Steve Waugh and Michael Bevan got among the runs later in the day to rescue our position and turn what started out as a disaster day for Australia into quite a pleasing one.

On the morning of the second day my wife Judi telephoned to tell me to hang in there. It was great to hear from her because I was feeling pretty ordinary. We ended up being bowled out for 337. Our tail failed to wag, which is not surprising when you're up against bowlers like Akram and Waqar Younis who make a habit of cleaning up the lower order. At the end of the day they were 7-209 after being 1-150 earlier. They were definitely in trouble but we had to pull out all stops to capitalise on their shaky position next day. In the dressing room there was a lot of talk about how our winning the game was just a formality. I knew I had to stamp out that complacency. The boys were talking as if winning the Test was only a matter of going out onto the field. I told them it was much too early to be counting our chickens just yet.

And so it proved. On day three we got them out for 256, which left us 81 ahead. Not bad, I thought. As I went out to open our second innings I pondered what AB would do in this situation and knew he would have gritted his teeth and nailed them. I resolved to really grind it into the Pakistanis. But the best-laid plans sometimes go awry, and this was the case that day when I snicked a slow ball from Waqar Younis to the keeper in the second over and was out for a duck again. It was a great debut as captain. As I walked off the field, much as I had after my first Test failure when I convinced myself I'd played my one and only game, I thought, 'Oh well, at least I've captained Australia for one Test.' At close of play that day we were 5-181, a handy lead of 262. We would have been in far better shape if Steve Waugh and Michael Bevan hadn't got first-ball ducks. They'd come in right after Boon and Mark Waugh had batted superbly to take us to 2-171 before Waugh fell. At his demise the Pakistanis went up a notch in intensity and blasted Steve and Michael out and turned the game around.

Day four saw us all out for 232 with Boon not out 114. The Pakistanis were left to score 313 in a day and a half. The match looked like going down to the wire. At stumps Pakistan were 3-157. We knew we needed some quick wickets on the final day but considered ourselves to be in good shape. With Warnie and Tim May there and the wicket turning a bit, you never know.

When we took the field that morning they needed to score 159 runs and we needed seven wickets. I'll quote here from notes I made at the end of that deciding day's play.

Well, it's 4 p.m. on the fifth day. I'm in my room, the captain who lost his first Test. But I don't know how. We did nearly everything right. We got the early breakthrough we needed. We had them at 9-258 needing another 56 to win. And they got the runs. Things didn't go our way. We had a couple of close LBWs given not out, had what we thought was a caught-behind given not out. At the end we had them at 9-311 with them requiring just three more runs for victory. Warnie was bowling to Inzamam-Ul-Haq who ran way down the wicket, swung and missed the ball which kept low. Heals missed the stumping and the ball went through his legs for four leg byes. Really, this was the Test match that got away. That's the best way I can sum it up. We did everything right and lost by a wicket . . . The score

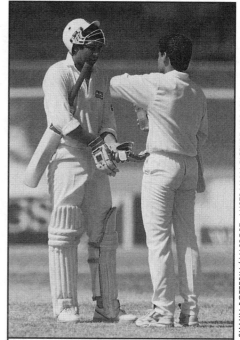

SHAUN BOTTERILL/ALLSPORT•AUSTRALIAN PICTURE LIBRARY

Inzamam-Ul-Haq takes a break during his match-winning innings of 58 not out in the first Test.

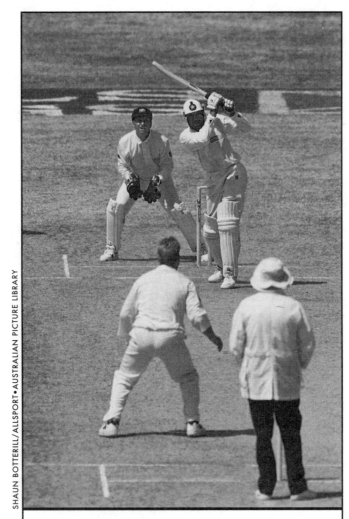

Zahid Fazal hits out for Pakistan in the first innings of the Karachi Test.

will read that Pakistan won by a wicket and Mark Taylor made a pair on debut as captain. In summary, though, I was happy with my game as captain. I followed my hunches and I'm proud to stand by them. I know there will be better games ahead for me with the bat and if I can get that right I think good days are ahead for this team as well.

PS: I think I've experienced just about every possible emotion — except for the thrill of a victory — that a captain can experience in one Test. A pair and a close loss are not the ideal ingredients for your first Test, but I have experienced the worst, so bring on the best.

I was clearly looking forward to the rest of my captaincy career.

I'll never forget the fighting spirit we showed in that roller coaster Test in which the ascendancy changed hands many times. We were the walking wounded for much of that match. Craig McDermott had missed the game with a

Opposing captains, Salim Malik and Taylor, before the start of the first Test against Pakistan.

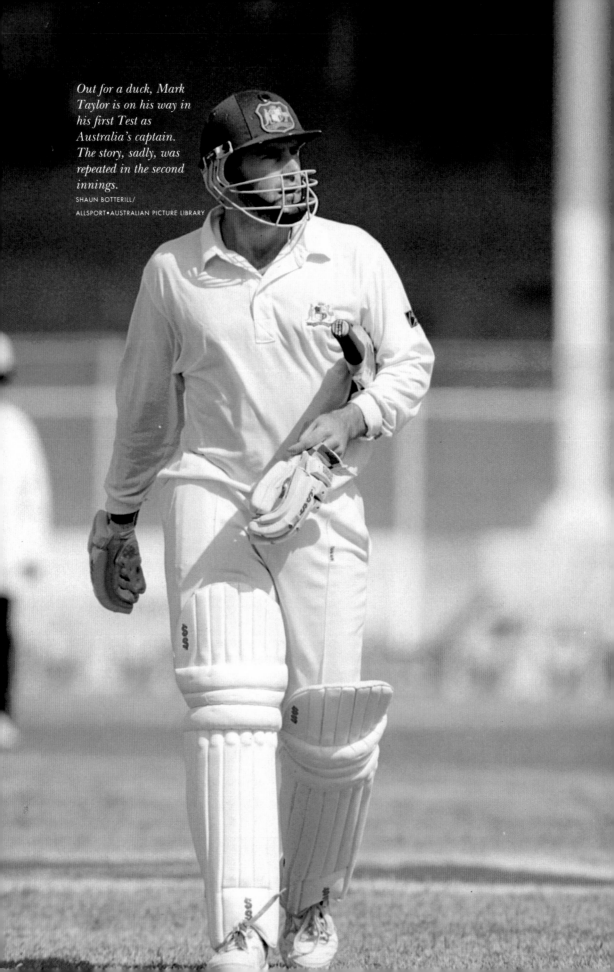

Out for a duck, Mark Taylor is on his way in his first Test as Australia's captain. The story, sadly, was repeated in the second innings.

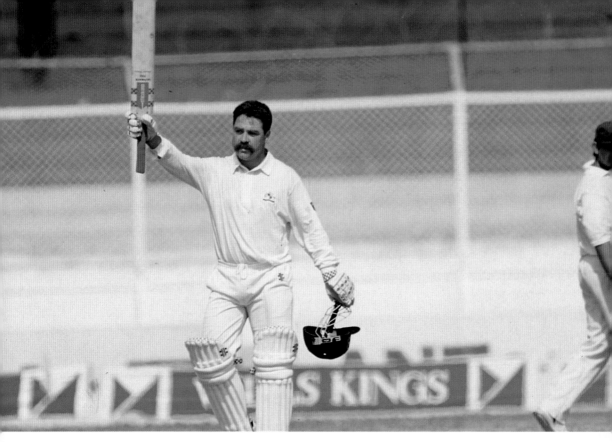

ABOVE *David Boon reaches his 100 in the second innings of the first Test against Pakistan in Karachi.*

SHAUN BOTTERILL/ALLSPORT•AUSTRALIAN PICTURE LIBRARY

BELOW *Salim Malik during his match-saving innings of 237 in the second Test.* SHAUN BOTTERILL/ALLSPORT•AUSTRALIAN PICTURE LIBRARY

ABOVE *Action during the second Test, Pindi Stadium, Rawalpindi.* SHAUN BOTTERILL/ALLSPORT•AUSTRALIAN PICTURE LIBRARY
BELOW *Michael Slater sets off during his first innings century in the second Test.* SHAUN BOTTERILL/ALLSPORT•AUSTRALIAN PICTURE LIBRA

Michael Bevan shows some of the form that gave him an aggregate of 243 runs, with an average of over 60 for the three Test series.

The Australian skipper, in casual mood on tour in Pakistan. SHAUN BOTTERILL/ALLSPORT•AUSTRALIAN PICTURE LIBRARY

An unusual sight – Mark Taylor, bowling during Pakistan's second innings of the second Test. Taylor and Michael Slater headed the bowling averages (Taylor 3-1-11-1 and Slater 1.1-0-4-1) for the Test series. SHAUN BOTTERILL/ALLSPORT•AUSTRALIAN PICTURE LIBRARY

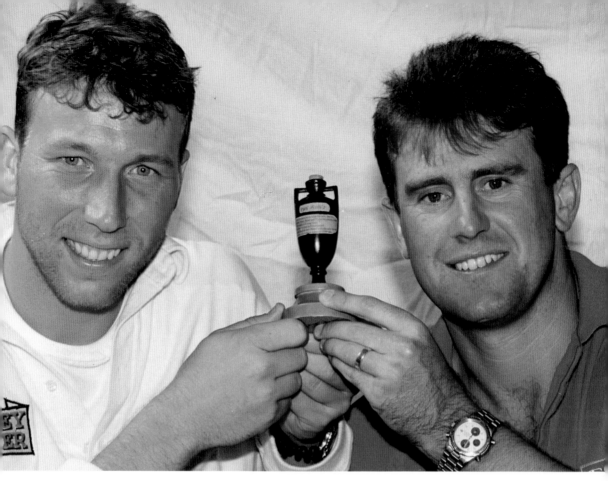

ABOVE *Atherton and Taylor and the most prized trophy in cricket.* BEN RADFORD/ALLSPORT•AUSTRALIAN PICTURE LIBRARY
BELOW *Craig White takes a magnificent one-handed catch to dismiss Steve Waugh off Tufnell in Australia's second innings at the Gabba.* BEN RADFORD/ALLSPORT•AUSTRALIAN PICTURE LIBRARY

ABOVE *Alec Stewart, bowled by Warne on the final day of the first Test, much to the delight of Healy and Taylor.*

BELOW *Darren Gough hits out against McDermott during his rapid fire first innings 51 in the Sydney Test.*

ABOVE *The well-publicised 'barmy army', which supported England with great gusto throughout their Australian tour.*

BELOW *Devon Malcolm is caught by David Boon off Warne to complete Warne's hat-trick in the second Test.* *azingly two Australian cricketers had completed hat-tricks in the space of 11 weeks (Fleming in Pakistan, Second Test).*

ABOVE *A happy Mike Gatting drenches his captain during the celebrations of the Adelaide victory over Australia.*
BEN RADFORD/ALLSPORT•AUSTRALIAN PICTURE LIBRARY

BELOW *Mike Atherton on the road to defeat, fifth Test, Perth.* BEN RADFORD/ALLSPORT•AUSTRALIAN PICTURE LIBRARY

Michael Slater shows his style, seen hooking in his innings of 124 in Perth, fifth Test.

GRAHAM CHADWICK/ALLSPORT•AUSTRALIAN PICTURE LIBRARY

ABOVE *Mark Taylor leads the way with a half century in the second of the limited over finals against Australia A at the MCG.* BEN RADFORD/ALLSPORT•AUSTRALIAN PICTURE LIBRARY

BELOW *The Australian team and their prize, the World Series Trophy, at the conclusion of the second final.*

BEN RADFORD/ALLSPORT•AUSTRALIAN PICTURE LIBRARY

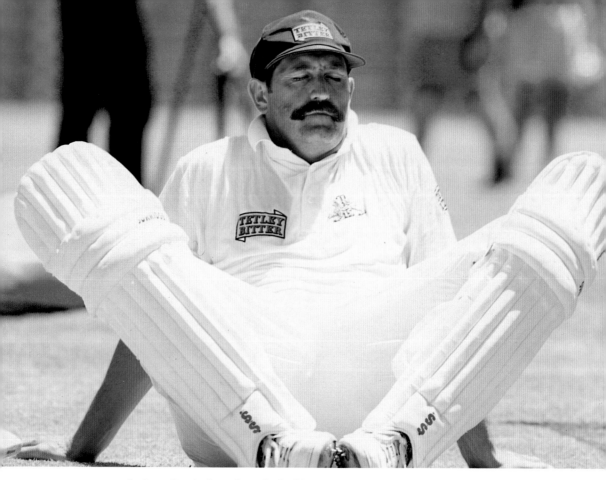

ABOVE *Graham Gooch, for so long the backbone of the English batting lineup, decided that this Ashes tour would be his last.* GRAHAM CHADWICK/ALLSPORT•AUSTRALIAN PICTURE LIBRARY

BELOW *The New Zealand team line up prior to the final against Australia at Eden Park.* ANDREW CORNAGA/AUSTRALIAN PICTURE LIBR.

bad toe injury. Glenn McGrath tore his hamstring during the game and couldn't bowl in the second innings. Tim May threw his neck out on the fourth day. Joey Angel and Steve Waugh took the second new ball. Angel and Warne were my only fit frontline bowlers. I'm sure we would have won the game if all our bowlers had been fit. To come so close to winning with such a depleted team was a great effort. For good reasons and bad, the first Test against Pakistan in 1994 taught me plenty about what it takes to be a captain. I learned that bad fortune is the ultimate test of you as a man and a skipper. You learn to keep fighting when all is falling apart around you. The day after the game I was so proud of my boys and looking eagerly forward to better days in the second Test to be contested in just two days time at Rawalpindi.

The Pakistan team celebrate their one-wicket victory over Australia in the first Test at Karachi.

We batted first and I was nervous as hell as Akram and Younis roared in to bowl at me. I had decided to attack half-volleys and anything short and be very positive, but early on all I could think was: 'I'm on my third duck.' Then I got off the mark when I pushed a ball on my hip forward to square leg and took a single. My first run of the series and my first run as captain. Thank goodness! I went on to make a pretty good 60 and the side notched 521. I was disappointed at my LBW dismissal to a guy called Moshin Kamal but I'd played a few hooks and cuts and drives and thought, 'This is more like it.' I was back in the run-scoring groove and was feeling more confident.

We got the Pakistanis out for 260 in their first dig, and that presented me with a major decision: 'Do I make them follow on, or do we bat again?' In hindsight it is easy to say that we should have batted on and made them bat in the last day and a half when Warnie would have made hay on what may have been a deteriorating pitch. But I didn't. I sent Pakistan in to follow on and we didn't make the most of our chances and let them off the hook. They had something like half an hour to bat on the third night and I set a trap for Aamir Sohail by putting two blokes at deep backward square leg anticipating his hook. He fell for the trap, hooking Jo Angel straight down Warnie's throat, but Warnie dropped the catch.

Next day by just after lunch we'd taken only one wicket and Salim Malik was batting. I said to Angel, 'Joey, Salim's looking pretty good. Why don't we try something different. We'll put two blokes out for the hook. I want you to bowl around the wicket into his ribs a bit, and then bowl the odd wide one and see if we can get him caught behind.' Joey did everything right. Bowled him a good bouncer first-up. The second ball was into his ribs, but he kept it out. The third was a bit wider and Salim nicked it straight to me at first slip — and I dropped the catch. He was on 20 then and went on to make 237. By the time we got him out the game had passed us by. If I'd caught that ball when he was on 20, they would have been 2-120, still 140 runs behind us and it would have been hard for them to recover from that. Cricket is the kind of game that can really tear your heart out. They ended up getting 537 and the game fizzled out into a boring draw. One bright ray of sunlight in that second Test was when Damien Fleming took a hat-trick late on the last day, including the long-overdue wicket of Malik.

The third Test at Lahore was also a disappointment. I lost the toss, which cost us the chance to bat first on a wonderful batting strip — no grass, very hard, very flat. Their two main strike bowlers, Wasim Akram and Waqar Younis, were out,

SHAUN BOTTERILL/ALLSPORT•AUSTRALIAN PICTURE LIBRARY

The Australian players show their anguish as the ball runs for 4 byes, giving Pakistan a sensational victory at Karachi.

Wasim Akram hits out during his innings of 45 not out in the Rawalpindi Test.

so it would have been ideal to go in first and build a huge score and then put the pressure on their batsmen as the wicket deteriorated. But I called wrongly and in they went. We dropped more catches and they made 373. They really took their time too, because being one-up in the series they were content to play for a draw. We replied to their first innings score with 455 which put us 82 ahead as we commenced our second dig. At one stage we had them at about 5-107, then our old nemesis Salim Malik hit 143 and saved the game for them. It was really Salim who killed us in that series.

As we returned home, having lost the series 1-0, I reflected that it could all have turned out so differently. We lost the first Test on the last ball of the day. Had we come out on top then and gone 1-0 up, Pakistan would have been more aggressive and not played for draws in the remaining Tests. I think we would have seen an outstanding series. But that's all academic, because the record books show that Australia still has not won a series in Pakistan in 35 years. The one consolation was the one-dayers. We played wonderfully well to beat Pakistan and South Africa and I was very happy with my form with the bat in the series. The final against Pakistan remains in my memory. What a game that was for us, and helped to erase many of the unhappier memories of that tour. It was at Lahore in front of a packed house. I scored a pretty good 56 and Michael Slater made 66 and suddenly we were about 120 from 25 overs. A score of 290 looked possible until we lost a few wickets and we reset our sights at 230 or so. Then in came Michael Bevan to blast 50-odd off 40 balls, hitting Younis and Akram for four after four. He played shots that only he can play, shots I can only dream about. It was one of the best short one-day innings I've witnessed. He took us to

269. The Pakistanis went into bat and this time we held our catches and put them under intense pressure. We got them out for 205 to win the one-day series. They're a top side and to down them convincingly on their home soil was great.

Pakistan is always interesting. Things tend to *happen* there. Certainly there were some rich incidents on our tour, but the one I remember most came during the one-day tournament. We were scheduled to play against Pakistan at Gujranwala, about an hour and half's drive from Lahore, so we piled onto the bus at 6 a.m. to be there in plenty of time for the 9.30 start. There had been torrential rain all night, but when we checked the local cricket association assured us the game was going ahead. Strange, I thought, because the roads were awash with water. Sure enough, when we arrived at the ground one end of the pitch was under water. There was no way any play could take place that day. Unfortunately, the Pakistani officials had already admitted many spectators for what was a big game and the ground was full. The crush was exacerbated by the fact that there had been some illegal tickets sold as well, so in some cases three people had turned up to claim the same seat. Prior to the official starting time there was a minor riot when a large body of ticket holders broke down a fence in their rush to get a seat. Some of the fans were trapped under the collapsed fence while others trampled over the top. Thanks to some swift action by security men who forced the crowd off the fence, and out onto the field, what could have been a major disaster was averted. One man fainted in the melee, there were a few minor injuries, and thankfully, that was about it.

After the crowd settled there was a three-hour delay as we waited for the wicket to dry. By midday the wicket was still nowhere near fit for play and the umpires were preparing to abandon the game. A Pakistani official came to me and declared that if there was no cricket, the crowd would kill us! We agreed to play a 15-over exhibition match, where the batting took place at the waterlogged end, just out of the crease. It was a slog-a-thon where we tried to hit as many sixes as we could. The crowd cheered both sides and went home reasonably happy. Thank God no-one was seriously injured.

Flying home, a kaleidoscope of memories played in my mind: my first-Test pair, our one-day triumph, the dropped catches, the pressure from the press. I knew I'd be a better skipper after that experience. And I thought too of the forthcoming Ashes series at home against England.

Chapter 5

THE WINNING
OF THE ASHES

I knew the 1994-95 Ashes series would break or make me as a captain. The Ashes are the most glittering prize in world cricket and are always fiercely contested. On the field there has never been any quarter given nor asked. English captain Mike Atherton came out at the beginning of the tour saying his men were going to play it hard and tough and if the Australians wanted to sledge then his men would not turn the other cheek. Happily, there were no ugly incidents in any Test and, in fact, the whole series was played in an excellent spirit. This was as much our doing as the Englishmen's.

I had only been home from Pakistan for four days when I turned out for New South Wales against England in Newcastle. Preparing for the game, I cast my mind back to the 1989 series when, after being branded the worst side to leave Australia, we met them in the first Test at Headingley. We were in trouble early after Boon and Marsh went cheaply. I was at the crease hanging in there as best I could when AB strode to the wicket and grabbed the game — and the series — by the scruff of the neck. He really took to the English bowlers and with a string of pulls and square cuts wrested the initiative from them. He scored 66, but more importantly he inspired me to score my first Test century. Then Steve Waugh took up where AB left off and whacked 177 not out. The Poms never recovered and we won the series 4-0. I learned that day the great psychological damage you can do with a strong first-up innings.

Now at Newcastle in 1994 I proposed to set a similar example to my men in our first encounter with the old enemy. I was glad to be facing big Devon Malcolm who had a huge wrap on him then and was threatening to match the speed and effectiveness of Lillee and Thommo in their prime. I took Devon from the start and hit 150 in less than a day. Mark Waugh made a good 80. In the second innings Mike Slater made 94 and I hit 47. Our aggressive and confident start against the Englishmen put them on the back foot and, like their 1989 counterparts, they never really reclaimed the initiative.

After winning the toss in the first Test in Brisbane we were 4-329 at stumps with Michael Slater scoring 176 in rapid time. We really attacked their bowlers, a task made a bit easier maybe by the fact that Malcolm missed the game with chicken pox. We picked up with the ball where we'd left off with the bat and blasted England out for only 167. That presented the big question: to make them follow on or to bat ourselves and turn Shane Warne and Tim May loose on them in the last innings. I was for batting ourselves and Ian Healy thought the same. Steve Waugh and Boonie wanted to stick the Poms in again and try to wrap up the match quickly. I thought hard and concluded that our best chance — with McDermott bowling beautifully but Glenn McGrath not at his top — was to bowl last and hope Warne and May would come into their own. So I didn't enforce the follow-on. We batted again and scored 248, setting them 508 to get in the last five sessions of play. England dug in and with Graham Thorpe and Graeme Hick playing well they went to 2-211 at the end of day four and I was worried. A draw looked probable. I called the guys together and said, 'Let's not

*Mark Taylor during his first Test innings on home soil. At the wicket
against the old enemy at Brisbane's Gabba.*

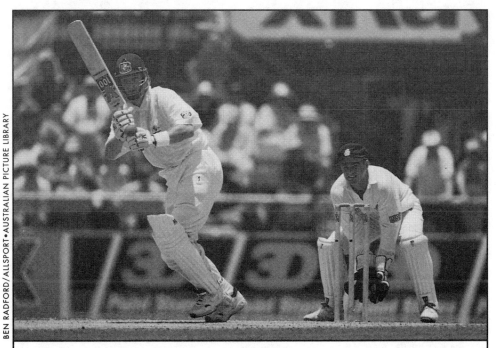

Mark Waugh was in full flight in his magnificent innings of 140 in the Gabba Test.

get frustrated or upset, let's just keep doing what we're doing and the breaks will come our way.' Early on the fifth day I took Warnie aside and told him, 'Just relax, just keep bowling as well as you can. Stay cool and things will go your way.' He admitted he was beginning to lose it a little but would knuckle down. His next ball to Thorpe was a low full toss, and the batsman missed it completely. Had he been in an aggressive frame of mind he would have belted it to the fence, but he was thinking about survival and he was caught in two minds. The ball hit the footmarks, spun back and bowled him. Graeme Hick, also playing a stout hand, was next to fall. Warnie bowled him a ball he tried to let go but it hit him on the pad, bounced up and hit his bat and was snapped up by Heals diving forward. That started a batting collapse and we had won the game by tea. Warnie had figures of 8-71.

Mike Atherton, LBW to Warne for 23 in England's second innings of the first Test. Warne returned match figures for the Gabba Test of 11 for 110.

At the press conference afterwards one journalist — I think it was Phil Wilkins — asked me what I said to Warnie before he bowled the ball that got Thorpe out. I replied, 'Oh, I told him to bowl a full toss because he's bound to miss it.' Anyone who knows the game would have known I was joking, but at least a couple of papers reported that I had ordered the full toss. I was also asked about my decision not to enforce the follow-on. If we hadn't won the game I would have been castigated for the decision, but as it turned out we did win and everyone praised me for such a wise choice. The essence of captaincy is making a decision and then sticking by it. Indecision is no way to win a cricket match.

May appeals unsuccessfully for the wicket of Atherton during the first Test.

Michael Slater reaches his 100 en route to 176 in the Test series opener.

For the second Test in Melbourne, which started on Christmas Eve, England selected their best side with Devon Malcolm returning after his bout of illness. They sent us in and at the end of the day had us in strife at 7-220 . We spent an uneasy Christmas rest day and even I put our chances of winning at only fifty-fifty. On Boxing Day we rounded off our innings at 279, saved only by Steve Waugh's 94 not out and a swashbuckling 16 to Damien Fleming. Then we came out and bowled the Poms out for 212. Warnie got 6-64 and Craig McDermott 3-72. In our second dig, Boonie made a good century on a wicket that was playing up and down a bit. With four sessions to go we were 380-odd ahead and that was always going to be too many runs for England to score on that wicket. At the end of Day 4 we had taken four English wickets and they were in real trouble — with Craig McDermott and Damien Fleming bowling beautifully. It was all over by lunch on the fifth day. We had bowled England out for only 92. Shane Warne took a hat-trick on that final morning in front of his home crowd to cap a marvellous victory for us. I remember thinking that things couldn't get much better. We were playing well, the Poms weren't, the third Test was coming up — and it seemed that the Ashes were all but retained.

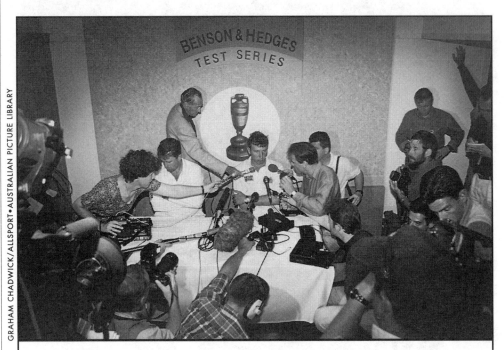

England captain Mike Atherton faces the media after Australia's win in the second Test in Melbourne.

We went from Melbourne straight to Sydney for the New Year's Day third Test. The press build-up to the match was all about how we were going to thrash this pathetic England side and win the series 5-0, how Mike Atherton had to be sacked and so on. England weren't listening. They won the toss and batted. At first it looked good for us when we had them about 3-20. I recall thinking, 'Wow, we're going to knock these blokes over for 150 at best and wrap up the series 3-0.' But Mike Atherton stood his ground and scored an excellent 88 in tough conditions, a fine captain's innings. John Crawley supported him with a good 70-odd. These two took England to 3-194 and looked to be settling in for big scores. Then with thirty minutes' play left I took the second new ball and at stumps they were 7-198. What a strange day's cricket it had been. We had taken three wickets in the first hour, four in the last half hour — and none in between.

On the second day, Darren Gough came out and smashed us, hitting 51. After being 3-20, they ended up making 309, a great comeback and a harbinger

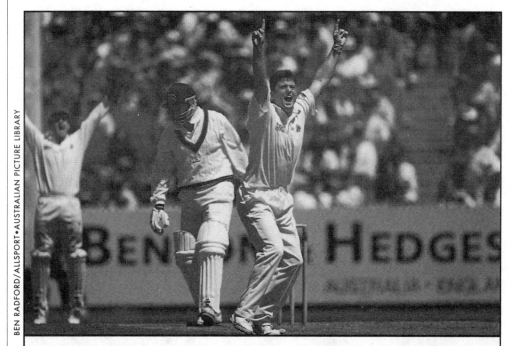

Darren Gough appeals without result for the wicket of Steve Waugh. Waugh had a fine Test, finishing not out in both innings (94 and 26).

of what lay ahead for us. When our innings began, Michael Slater and I were cruising at 0-12 when Slats got out and that started a collapse of major proportions. At lunch we were 6-57. I was 19 not out and remember thinking, 'I'm going to carry my bat through this innings and I'm going to make about 30.' After lunch the rot continued with Warne and May going cheaply. It was left to Craig McDermott and me to hold the fort. We needed 116 to avoid the follow-on. Devon Malcolm granted us both a reprieve when he dropped a hard caught-and-bowled chance off me and couldn't quite pick up a ball that Craig skied towards him at mid-on. After a few risky singles we averted the follow-on, but I was out for 49, caught and bowled by a slower delivery from Darren Gough. Then Damien Fleming made a first ball duck and we were left lamenting a total of 116. The Poms went into bat and did it easy, setting us 440-odd in four sessions and half an hour to win the game.

Devon was bowling really sharp on a belter of a pitch. I remember getting hit on the gloves. I remember too thinking that here I had to stand up and be counted as captain: 'If I get out I won't go down fending a ball around the corner or to the gully, I'll get out playing my shots.' So Devon bowled me a wide one and I slashed at it, nicking it over fourth slip to the fence for four. His next ball was short — somehow I knew it would be — and I despatched that for four too. In his next over I drove him off the back foot through the covers for another boundary and hooked him to the fence a few balls later. At tea, after eight overs, I was 29. Slats was 7. By stumps I had settled down as I always do and

Slats had caught up to me as he always does. We were both around 70 at the end of play and Australia was 0-139.

When we took the field on the last day of that remarkable Test we needed 310 runs to win and we had our full complement of wickets to get them. There was a buzz around the ground as the 25,000-strong crowd and both teams anticipated a great day's cricket. I'd sat down with the guys in the dressing room before and asked the boys, 'OK, how are we going to attack this?' and to a man they said we should go for a win, rather than just try to preserve our wickets and play for a draw. To have won that match after being all out for 116 in the first innings would have been something to tell the grandchildren. England bowled very well indeed all morning, and very tightly. Scoring was tough, but Slats made his hundred just before lunch and I was 94.

Graeme Hick and Ian Healy watch as the ball trickles onto the stumps, but the bails stay put. Third Test.

To win we needed 240 runs in two sessions, or sixty overs. At lunch we all believed a win was possible and that with ten wickets still in hand we would give it a real go. Four runs an over are gettable if you hustle. Then the heavens opened during lunch and ruined what should have been a mighty conclusion to the Test. The rain cost us eight overs and when we finally went back onto the field the wicket was greasy. There was no way we could have got the required runs on that strip without running a big risk of losing all our wickets. After all, the bottom line was we didn't have to win that game to wrap up the Ashes, as we were ahead in the series. I told the boys to play for a draw. First-up Slats played a poor shot to Angus

Fraser and Phil Tufnell took a fine catch. I scored my century — in the conditions I rate it my finest Test hundred — before being bowled by Devon Malcolm for 113.

All the time it was drizzling and the wicket was getting harder and harder to play on. Things had taken on a dangerous edge for us. Next Boonie was caught in slips and we were on the skids. Steve and Mark Waugh went quickly. Michael Bevan, who had struggled all series, was caught behind and suddenly we were five or six wickets down. The only safety net for us was that it was getting dark. Play was extended an extra hour because of the time lost during the day to rain, but the poor light resulted in the umpires forbidding England to use their fast bowlers for fear of harming the batsmen. If Mike Atherton had persisted in bowling Malcolm and Fraser the umpires would have offered us the opportunity to call it quits because of the light and, believe me, we would have taken them up on it. The fact that they were not able to bowl their quicks, with the new ball just ten overs old, saved our lives. As it happened, Warne and May defied the slower English bowlers for an hour and at stumps it was 7-344. We were 100-odd runs short of a win, but we still had three wickets in hand and so gratefully accepted a draw. We had retained the Ashes at least by holding a 2-0 lead in the series with two games to go. The best England could hope for was a tied series if they won the remaining Tests in Adelaide and Perth.

After Adelaide that scenario was a distinct possibility. The Test was a major disappointment for us. Nor, in my opinion, was it really a great game of cricket. England prevailed over a run of bad luck to win against the odds. They went

Devon Malcolm shows Mark Waugh the way after having him caught by Rhodes for 3, in the third Test.

into the game without the big-hearted Darren Gough, a real star of the future, who had a stress fracture in his foot. Graeme Hick was out too with a back problem. The match was ours on a plate, but we lost it. They won the toss and by stumps had powered along to 2-196, helped again by our not taking our chances and putting down at least four catches. We fought our way back into the game on Day 2, wrapping up their innings for 353 — a good effort after the events of the first day. Following our first innings of 419 in which Greg Blewett made a brilliant century on debut we had manoeuvered ourselves into a good position by the end of the fourth day. We had them 6-220 in their second innings, a lead of only 154 runs. With the wicket playing well and most of our batsmen in form an Aussie victory looked highly probable. However, the Poms — and especially Phil DeFreitas — had other ideas. Phil scored a quickfire 88 on the final morning of the match and changed the game. What had looked a comfortable assignment on Day 4 had turned into a chase after 248 runs in the last two sessions of the match. We decided to go after the runs — much to our ultimate grief. Both Slats and I were out early to Devon Malcolm, who bowled very fast that day. Unfortunately this set the pattern — and with six overs to go our last wicket fell. We were all out for 156. On the last day we had to score 263. At the end of the match, which frankly we weren't expecting to lose, we were only 2-1 up with a Test to play. The Englishmen had their tails up and were looking forward to the fifth Test in Perth to square the series.

Mike Atherton shows his appreciation for the man of the hour, Devon Malcolm, after Malcolm's match-winning performance in the fourth Test at Adelaide for England.

*Phil DeFreitas hits out during his knock of 88 in the second innings. DeFreitas'
contribution turned the Test match around.*

*Mike Gatting pulls to the boundary during his first innings of 117
in the fourth Test.*

BEN RADFORD/ALLSPORT•AUSTRALIAN PICTURE LIBRARY

One of the few pluses to come out of the Adelaide Test was Greg Blewett's outstanding debut. Blewett is seen here during his innings of 102 not out.

GRAHAM CHADWICK/ALLSPORT•AUSTRALIAN PICTURE LIBRARY

Phil Tufnell shows his delight after taking a catch to dismiss Slater off Malcolm for 5. Second innings, fourth Test.

Before we headed west I had to attend to some urgent family business back in Sydney. My wife was to give birth by caesarean section to our second child, and the operation was scheduled for 8 a.m. on the morning following the Adelaide Test. After the post-match press conference I raced to the airport and flew home on a late evening flight. Judi was already in hospital, so I spent the night at home, barely sleeping at all. I think I managed only about two hours sleep, so nervous was I about the operation. I was troubled too by our disappointing loss to England. I arrived at the hospital at 7a.m., a bundle of nerves, unlike Judi who was quite relaxed. I went with her to the operating theatre, the plan being that I would sit with her through the surgery. I have to confess that I was no hero. Before the operation started I was feeling clammy, then when it was in progress I felt decidedly sick. I thought I was going to faint. Meanwhile Judi was laughing and chatting to me as the doctors tugged and pulled, trying to get the baby out. I had to leave the room. I was sitting in the waiting room, worried as hell and feeling queasy, when the obstetrician called out, 'Come back in, we're about to get your baby out.' I went back in and right on cue out came Jack, our second son. I was so proud and happy. I remembered back to the birth of our first son, William, in 1992 and how great a moment it was for me and how I'd shed a tear when I first held him in my arms. That was one of the greatest — if not *the* greatest — highlights in my life and the feeling when Jack was born was just as good. Suddenly cricket and our fourth-Test loss meant nothing to me. That afternoon I had to carry out another pressing family task: to organise a birth certificate for Jack, because Judi and both the boys were to accompany me to New Zealand for our short tour there on February 13, just a fortnight away. That done, I hurried back to the hospital, made sure Judi and Jack were doing fine, drove home to pack my cricket gear and suit, then caught a plane for Perth and our date with the Poms.

As I crumpled into my seat in the plane I was pretty knackered, as you might imagine. It had been quite a day. I was sound asleep before the plane took off. When I awoke one of the flight hostesses approached and asked how I was doing. 'Yeah, good thanks,' I replied.

'Congratulations,' she said, then, 'I hear you've just had a child. Can I get you a drink?' Could she what! I introduced myself to the passenger sitting next to me and for the next four hours we drank champagne and I told her all about childbirth. Fortunately, she didn't know much about cricket and that suited me fine, because cricket was the last thing I wanted to talk about. I knew I should have been sleeping, but I was too hyped up and bubbling about being a dad for the second time. I'm sure I bored the hell out of my travelling companion talking about Judi and the kids, but we arrived at Perth feeling happy, probably down to the fact that we'd fuelled our flight with all that champagne and red wine. It was a memorable journey, and a precursor to a memorable Test match.

The fifth Test in Perth was a complete turnaround. In Perth we won the toss and batted, and with the help of some slipshod catching by the Poms we

amassed 402. When it was our turn to
bowl, unlike in Adelaide we held our
catches and dismissed them for 295
giving us a handy first innings lead.
Thanks to a magnificent century by Greg
Blewett in our second innings, his second
in his first two Tests — a rare feat — we
were able to set them an 'impossible'
target of 453 over the final four sessions.
Craig McDermott and Glenn McGrath
both bowled superbly. When McDermott
disturbed Devon Malcolm's furniture just
after lunch on the final day we had won
the series, 3-1 — and retained the Ashes.

Mark Waugh, acting as a runner for
an injured Craig McDermott, is
tragically run out for 6, leaving brother
Steve stranded on 99 not out,
in the WACA Test.

Personally I had a good series, making
471 runs at an average of 47. I managed
to make a good contribution to our total
in all the Tests except Melbourne where I
did not play well. I felt good throughout
that summer and had captained my team
to an Ashes victory and to a win in the one-dayers as well, where we were up
against England, Zimbabwe and Australia A, the second-string Aussie side.

I had a problem with the Australia vs Australia A concept from the start. The
night before our first match against each other in Adelaide, the players from
both teams had a gathering at the Park Royal Hotel. We're all mates and were
talking and laughing and having a good time, knowing we'd be opponents next
day. But strangely, out there on the field, there was an ultra-competitive attitude
by blokes of both teams, spurred on by the crowd who were predominantly
barracking against Australia and supporting the underdog, Australia A, who were
pepped up and firing. We won by only a handful of runs after Glenn McGrath
took a good haul of their wickets right at the end. We won, but probably didn't
deserve to. I didn't enjoy the game. I don't enjoy playing against my team-mates.
To me it was like a trial game and I'm never at my best in trials.

Of course, it gave the Australia A guys a chance to break into the Australian
team, but to me the focus of the summer was on beating the Poms in the Tests
and winning the World Series, not beating our own Australian mates. I really
thought the Australian side had nothing to gain from the idea. The press and the
public took my comments the wrong way, as meaning I wanted the A team
disbanded. I didn't say that. Australia A added a lot to the competition. The
crowds for their fixtures were great. They played a good brand of cricket. They
made 264 against England in Sydney, which put the Poms on the rack, by forcing
them to make 230-or-so to qualify for the final on run rate, which they just failed
to do. The fact that Greg Blewett is now playing for Australia is the result of his

The two captains, presentation ceremony at the WACA after the fifth Test.

Craig McDermott takes a pearler to get rid of dangerman Gooch, caught and bowled for 4 in the second innings of the WACA Test.

THE WINNING OF THE ASHES

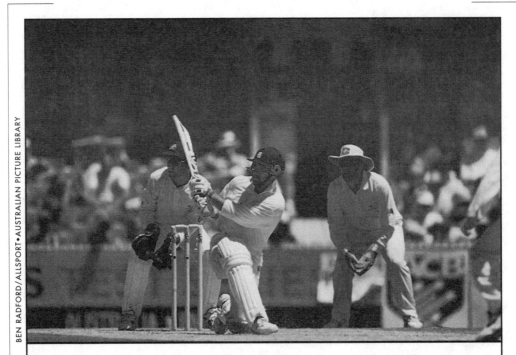

Graham Thorpe plays one of many forceful shots in his innings of 123 out of a team total of 295 at the WACA.

The Zimbabwe team, awaiting a decision from the 'third umpire'. The Zimbabweans did not set the world on fire, but gained valuable experience from the tour.

The English team in (fancy dress) party mood.

*Graeme Hick showed his class contributing 91 to help England defeat Australia
at the MCG, during the limited overs series.*

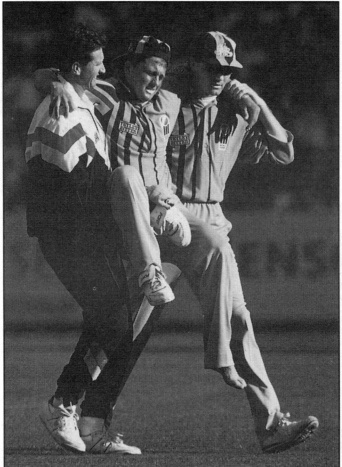

A sad sight for England as Dave Roberts and Shaun Udal carry
Darren Gough off the ground, during the one-dayer against
Australia at the MCG on 10/1/95. Gough had suffered
a stress fracture of the foot.

good performances for Australia A. Blokes like Ricky Ponting also got a wealth of experience playing international matches under lights in front of huge crowds.

Against our fellow Australians in the finals series, I lost the toss in both matches and they batted first, always an advantage in Sydney and Melbourne where the games were played. In both cities the wickets get slower, and harder to bat on, as the game goes on. Nevertheless we won both games. In the first we held them to 209 and overhauled them with five wickets to spare. In the second we held them to 226 and thanks to me, Slats and a good 50 by Steve Waugh we got the runs with an over to spare. This gave us an unbeatable 2-0 lead in the three-match series. They were two quality finals and the crowd certainly got its money's worth. But I don't think the Australia vs Australia A idea really captured the public's imagination. In Melbourne 57 000 people turned up to watch us, but if we'd been playing England I'm sure the crowd would have been 70-80 000.

Steve Waugh, 56 not out guides Australia to victory in the second final.

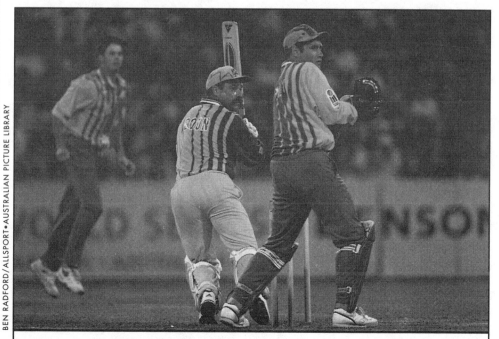

David Boon in action in the second World Series final at the MCG against Australia A.

That summer at home was a satisfying one for me. I achieved my aim to win the Ashes and the World Series. But it certainly flew by. Looking back, I can't believe how quickly the summer passed. There always seemed to be so much for me to do. As skipper you're up to your neck in every game you play, there's never a chance to relax and switch off. There were demands on me from the media, from the ACB — even on my off-days there were people wanting my time for a photo or a comment or an autograph or a chat about the game. I enjoyed every moment of it and wouldn't change a thing.

After the fifth Test in Perth I had four days at home before taking the Australian team to New Zealand for a one-day tournament involving us, the Kiwis, India and South Africa. Thankfully, after our red-hot Ashes summer, it was a relaxed campaign. We took our families along, we didn't practise much, we had a bit of fun and let our hair down generally. In spite of all this we beat New Zealand in the final, bowling them out for 137. My only disappointment was not carrying on for a century in our first game against the Kiwis. I reached 97 before being caught. I am still to make a century in a one-day match. As I write, I have thirteen Test hundreds to my name, but not a single one-day ton. That's a monkey on my back I'm very keen to knock off.

Mark Taylor lifts one over mid off during his innings of 44 in the New Zealand centenary One Day Final at Auckland.

PART 2

BATTLE IN THE CARIBBEAN —

West Indies Tour, 1995

Chapter 1

EARLY DAYS IN PARADISE

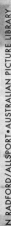

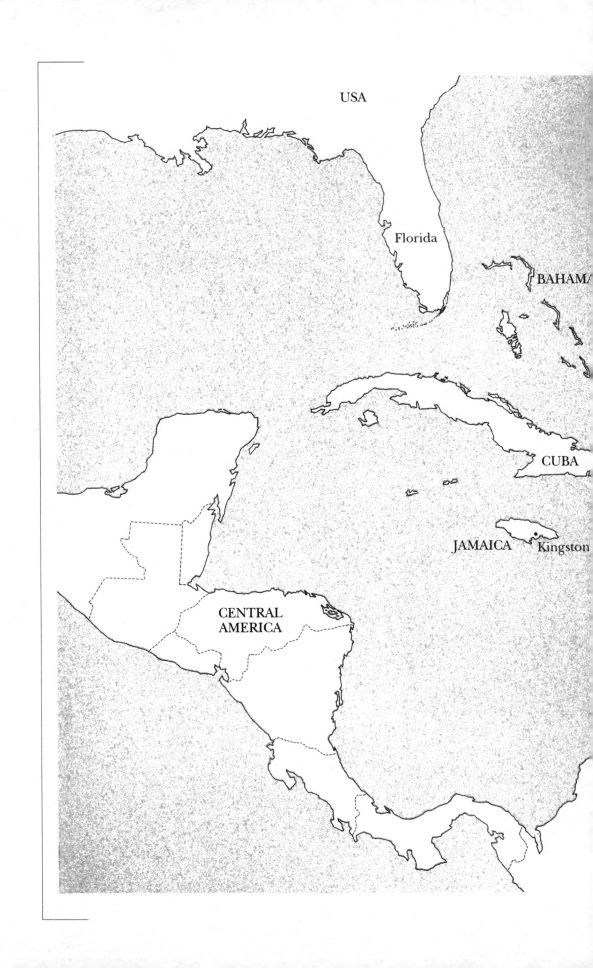

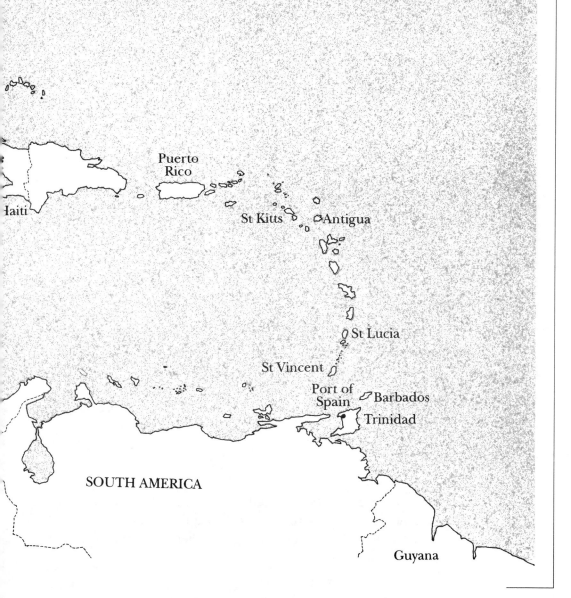

THE CAPTAIN'S LOG

TUESDAY, FEBRUARY 28

For me, the first day is always one of the toughest. I well remember the start to my first tour with the Australian team, to England in 1989. Judi and I had been married only three weeks then, and saying goodbye wasn't easy. I thought at the time it was one of the saddest days of my life. It hasn't got any easier since. Now that the Taylor family has grown with the arrival of William and Jack, that first day — the beginning of a tour, the stumbling through final goodbyes — has got even tougher. It really is a great wrench to leave your family, realising you won't see them again for a couple of months. I know that after today I'll never forget the look on the face of my eldest son, William. I was waving, and he was waving and he had that little teary look in his eye like he knew I wasn't going to be back for a long while. Now that he's nearly

Mark Taylor at home with William, getting ready for the West Indies tour.

three he's understanding a whole lot more about me. And when he sees the big suitcase packed alongside the 'coffin' in which my cricketing gear is laid out, he knows that Dad is going away again. Today was a sad one. I choked back a few tears, and I'm sure we all did . . .

Today, sadness and all, a regulation departure. A press conference at the airport at midday, and a chance to share some final thoughts on what lay ahead. Then a 1.40 p.m. flight with Cathay Pacific to Hong Kong. We had a three-hour stopover there, and the cards were out for a game of Five Hundred in the Marco Polo Lounge.

Heals and I sat aside for a while to talk about how we're going to tackle this tour. Second night in London we'll meet as a team to officially begin the talking and the planning. But today he and I got things rolling. We were in full agreement that we were to treat this as any other tour — even if it *was* the West Indies we were facing. We've played these guys plenty of times. And at times in the past there has been too much emphasis at our end on their fast bowlers and how lethal and quick they can be. My gut feeling, and Heals agreed, is that if we go about playing our cricket exactly as we have against the other teams we faced this year then there's no reason at all we can't win the series this tour.

I sense that the feeling in the side is very, very good. All the guys seem very relaxed, very happy — and genuinely looking forward to the challenge. We know it's going to be tough. At the back of my mind is the memory of 1991, the hardest tour I have ever been involved with — and that includes our struggles through Pakistan. The enjoyment factor is a big thing this time. I want everyone to stay happy, enjoy their cricket and enjoy the touring. Any falling off in the enjoyment factor inevitably has its effect on the playing field.

Flying on through the night to London, my mind wandered back to the press conference in Sydney. I took some encouragement out of that. It seemed to me that the media collectively were in a very buoyant mood. There were a lot of questions, many more than I thought I'd get, and a lot of them were good and positive. It was almost as if the press had straightaway tapped into the feeling within the team — that we can win this tour. Sitting in the darkened plane I felt good about that. And I ran through my mind again the need for the senior brigade — Heals and David Boon and Steve Waugh and Simmo (coach Bob Simpson) and myself — to keep that good spirit rolling. I know we have the personnel to win . . . but in the West Indies you need a lot more than just the right people.

MARCH 1

We made it. A fourteen-and-a-half-hour flight from Hong Kong, and the welcome sight of the lights of Heathrow, London, at 6 a.m. I managed seven or eight hours' sleep on the long haul over, and I'm feeling pretty fresh. The weather which greeted us, however, was not a lifter of spirits. Ten degrees, overcast and raining — a typical London greeting. We bussed in to a familiar base — the Westbury Hotel in Mayfair where we had stayed during the last two Ashes campaigns, 1989 and '93. It was good to get moving again and I spent the morning in the gym with Michael Slater, Errol Alcott, Craig McDermott, Justin Langer and Maysie (Tim May).

For lunch we renewed acquaintance with an old stamping ground — the Windmill pub, up the road. I think all of us were flagging as the afternoon wore on. We had a meeting planned for dinner time, but by late afternoon most of us were absolutely gone. I know I was — dog-tired and ready for bed. The meeting could wait, we decided.

MARCH 2

A great night's sleep. I was in bed by 5.30, awake at 4 a.m., then dozed off again until about 8 o'clock. After breakfast and another light session at the gym with Errol, Justin and Glenn McGrath I was feeling pretty close to top of the world. We're in London, so a bit of shopping was always going to be on the agenda, and after a sandwich at lunchtime a few of us hit the shops in a pretty modest way. I bought a pair of jeans, that's all, so it was no spree.

David Boon, Ricky Ponting and I had a beer in a pub close the hotel, and talked some cricket. Again the subject was very much the question of our *approach* to the tour and it was good that Ricky was there. We talked to him about the need for him to play his natural game, and for him to just get on with playing cricket the way he plays it. As we told Ricky, the West Indians' approach is based on setting out to make you change your game, to unsettle you. Ours is that there is no need to change the way we do things. Ricky is a good player, a good talent — and to change his game might be to change his future. He doesn't need to do that.

We were a fresher, fitter bunch tonight when we sat down for our team meeting. In what I had to say I pushed the enjoyment factor — and my sincere wish that I wanted to see the guys enjoying their cricket, and enjoying the tour. I called for us to challenge both their batting and bowling as we would against England or Pakistan or whoever. I honestly believe that our best chance of winning is to just treat the West Indians the way we treat any other side. In the past we have fallen into the trap of overrating them, falling for the hype and the psych-out tactics that go with any West Indian tour. I hope we can change that. We've got two months to find out.

The team meeting went very well. There was a lot of positive input from different people. Boonie and Mark Waugh in particular had some good things to say. I turned to Mark, who has a great record against the Windies, and he mentioned some simple things about batting against them. Like how much easier it gets after the first half-hour. How you can get used to the pace then, get used to the way they bowl. Mark admitted frankly that it was never easy for him in that first half hour, but after that things could click, and the bowling had a similarity about it which you could adjust to.

It was a quiet night for the team — with the prospect ahead of the flight to Barbados, and the real beginning of it all. An Indian meal up the road at a place called GayLords at Mayfair then back for some TV, watching the Dural Open, via SkySports. My mind tracked through the events of our meeting. The trick, I'm sure, is to stay fresh, and to enjoy what we're doing. If we can manage those things, we're in with a chance of winning.

MARCH 3

An early start. The wake-up call came at 5.45 a.m. for us to be at Gatwick in time to catch the 9.45 a.m. flight to Barbados. What a morning in London — one degree above freezing and the news that it had snowed overnight in the outlying suburbs. In Barbados when we touched down after an eight-hour flight it was twenty-nine degrees, with a humidity of eighty per cent.

Arriving earlier than expected, we almost caught West Indies officialdom on the hop. On our original itinerary we weren't due in until about 4.30 p.m. But because we'd taken an earlier flight than planned we were on the tarmac at Barbados at 2.25. In the circumstances it wasn't a big welcome — no pomp or ceremony. But it was a warm and genuine welcome all the same, from the former test opener Cammie Smith, who has generally looked after us over here, the Minister for Sport and a member of the Australian High Commission.

Then my first press conference in the West Indies. Just as it had been at Mascot all those kilometres away, this was a happy and even fairly enjoyable event, with the local press pretty buoyant and obviously looking forward to the series. There is expectation everywhere that it will be close and hard-fought, and I'm sure it will. I expressed the hope that if we could produce some good cricket along the way it would be good for us, and good for the game.

Barbados. We're certainly happy to be here. I think it's about the best place to stay in the West Indies and the resort club-hotel where we're staying — Club Rockley — is more than adequate. There's a nine-hole golf course ringing the hotel, good food, a nice beach. It's got everything going for it. I sense that spirits are sky-high. The feeling in the side at the moment is outstanding. The guys are very positive — looking forward to the series, looking forward to playing our brand of cricket. Things couldn't be better.

At the back of my mind, however, is the reality. That this is the calm before the storm. Things are going to get very tough, very quickly. The test for the team will come in places such as Jamaica and Guyana. We all know that and we're building nicely towards the challenges. Meanwhile some enjoyment — via nine holes on Club Rockley's convenient layout.

At this afternoon's press conference with the Aussie media, Phil Wilkins (*Sydney Morning Herald*), who knows us, and the game, so very well, made the point that he had tried to pick a one-day side, but had all sorts of trouble trying to reduce it below thirteen players. Wilko had thirteen 'certainties' in his team, and that's encouraging for us. It showed that in the perception of a bloke who knows cricket well that there is strength and depth in this team. I agree with him. It's going to be a tough selection tour. My hope is that come first Test time and, more importantly, come *last* Test time, we've still got thirteen or fourteen or even fifteen guys still pressing very hard for spots.

Tonight a relaxed and enjoyable Bajun-style reception around the pool. There was a band and a few nibblies and a few drinks. Informal, relaxed, enjoyable. The serious business is getting close, but we're easing nicely into the tour. Team harmony is fine, and so is the spirit.

MARCH 4

A small milestone this morning — the first practice of the tour. I was out of bed very early, jogging around the golf course, thanks to the time clock in my head not having quite adjusted yet. By the time we left for practice at nine o'clock I had been up for four hours. We trained from 9.30 to 12.30 and it was a good session. The guys were keen and sharp, and just about everyone seemed in pretty fair form. The half-hour fielding session at the end was done sharply and quickly, and everyone seemed to be enjoying it. I suppose we should be in good form. We haven't had a lot of cricket recently but we've had plenty over the last six months. If it happened that we *weren't* in form now it would probably be all too late.

A *big* plus to come out of the training session was the chance I had for a chat with Sir Garfield Sobers, the legendary Barbados and West Indian all-rounder who was down at the ground watching us work out. It was interesting to get his views on this current West Indies side. During a short break we took when a rain shower swept over the ground he told me that in his view the West Indies, at the moment, were not quite the team they used to be. I took that on board, but I told him I knew they had one great strength — that they were not used to losing and because of that adverse situations seemed to bring out the best in them. Sir Garfield of course realises that, but it seemed to me that he really believes they are ripe for the picking. It was good to see him. I remember another day in his company, when he was in Sydney coaching Mosman, and I had made 160 or so in a grade match. He was a special player and he's an interesting man — and I valued the chance to get together with him today.

There was a nice finish to the day's exercise — a session down at the beach at which we went through some stretches before taking to the water. We caught a few waves and had a bit of a run, and it was good.

Tomorrow the serious business begins. We play the Barbados Second XI — the reason for that being that their first team is away playing in the final of the one-day competition against Leeward Islands in Antigua. It's not the ideal preparation for us, but as I said, we've had a lot of cricket to ready us for all that

Sir Garfield Sobers and Mark Taylor discuss the meaning of life and other cricketing matters.

lies ahead, so we should be okay. I'll be watching from outside the fence, along with Mark Waugh, Glenn McGrath and Shane Warne, but the thing I know about this Australian team is that whoever we put on the park is thoroughly capable of doing the job. Especially in one-day cricket.

BEN FADFORD/ALLSPORT•AUSTRALIAN PICTURE LIBRARY

Mark Taylor in pensive mood at the second limited over international at Trinidad —
Australia's only success in the tournament.

CLIVE MASON/ALLSPORT•AUSTRALIAN PICTURE LIBRARY

David Boon, in practice mode for whatever lay ahead.

EARLY DAYS IN PARADISE

The day finished quietly. A meal in the Cloud Nine restaurant in the hotel and a beer or two while we listened to a local reggae band. And then to bed, with some butterflies . . . knowing that the serious stuff was about to begin.

MARCH 5

Well, we're off and running. Not a great game today — a mix of good and bad moments. We batted first and made 330 off our fifty overs, but Michael Slater went in the first over of the day and that was a blow. He's one bloke who hasn't had much cricket, due to a broken thumb having kept him out of the tour of New Zealand. So Steve Waugh, at three, was in bright and early — and he and Greg Blewett proceeded to put on 170 in about thirty overs, really smashing them about. Finally we had to retire Steve because he looked like he'd *never* get out. He played beautifully, hooks, pulls . . . the lot. The fact that he was so strong on the leg side showed that his confidence is really up. It has always been regarded as something of a weakness, the fact that he was often reluctant to play the pull shot, but today he brought out the entire array, and it was a great sign for us for what lies ahead.

Greg Blewett made 78 and batted very, very well. He played the way he had in the last two Tests in Australia — really attacked the bowling. Boonie made 70 and Justin Langer a good-looking 20. Except for Slats, who could have done with some more time at the wicket, it couldn't have gone better.

But our bowling fell short of what we had hoped for. The locals came out and scored 278 in their fifty overs, and our fast blokes bowled quite poorly. Craig McDermott and Damien Fleming were the two men we had wanted to do well. They both missed the New Zealand tour through injury and are now fit and healthy again — but the fact was they just didn't bowl well. That's always a chance when there is a combination of the sort of elements that were in today's game: a good wicket, a smallish field, a quick outfield and a team going for runs — which the Barbados side certainly did. But both McDermott and Fleming bowled a bit leg-stumpish . . . and paid the price. Their figures tell the story: McDermott 1/58, Fleming 1/56.

Both are smart enough to put it down to experience. I'm sure the message was pretty well instilled in Craig already that the wickets here are generally pretty flat with close boundaries and quick outfields — and if you don't bowl good line and length you'll go for a lot of runs . . . and a lot of quick runs.

Tim May bowled well. He got three wickets and went for 50-something, but he bowled pretty well. The fielding was average — at times downright poor and at other times pretty sharp. It wasn't a game to get excited about. But we're off the mark, the tour is underway, and there was enough good to counteract the bad.

Tonight we headed to an English-style pub called the Ship Inn to have a couple of beers and talk about the game. There was a good deal of talk about a bloke with the Christian names Patterson Thomson who played against us today. The 'Patterson' is after Patrick Patterson, the West Indies former fast bowler, and the 'Thomson' after Jeff Thomson, our own home-grown tornado. He was a big raw bloke with some genuine pace. His first ball to Michael Slater was a beamer which went straight over Slats' head and through on the full to the keeper who was some twenty-five metres back. The next was a fullish ball, well wide, and the third, as it turned out, a rare on-line delivery, shortish and rising, which Slater fended off and was caught.

The good news, however, about Patterson Thomson was that Steve Waugh, striding in very early at No. 3, just teed off and put him — and all the rest of the bowlers — in their place. That was a great sign. There are going to be times just like this through the tour when someone is bowling really quick, and when things are looking nasty. But the Steve Waugh response today was a message for the whole tour. After that shaky start his innings was a message: 'Look, we're here with a fair dinkum challenge. We're ready to play.' It was a nice bit of psychology, and something we've got to keep up.

MARCH 6

This morning we had three hours of practice in steamy conditions at Kensington Oval and I must say that I hit the ball pretty bloody ordinary. After leaving yourself out of a day's play as I did yesterday you need to have a good hit. I was looking forward to a good net session, but I struggled. Fortunately we've got another hit tomorrow before we head into the first one-day International and I'm hoping I'm going to strike the ball better tomorrow. I'm not too worried; I've been in pretty good form through the season and I shouldn't have lost all of that.

It's summertime conditions, and the living is pretty easy. Down at the beach this afternoon Heals and Justin Langer and I played this kind of racquetball game they go for over here. It was a nice leisurely afternoon, a couple of swims and a bit of a play-around. But life got more complicated when I headed back to the hotel, planning to watch a tape of the West Indies in action in New Zealand. I was keen to get a good look at a couple of their younger players, particularly the opening batsmen Stuart Williams and Sherwin Campbell, whom I haven't seen much of. But the technology beat me. Our VCR isn't working — and it's the only one in the joint. The tape will have to wait.

Tonight a pleasant sojourn as guests of Bob Witty, the Australian High Commissioner, at a barbecue at his residence at Sandy Bay, across on the western side of Barbados. After a few beers it was back to the hotel, and a chance to run through some thoughts about how things were going — and what lies ahead. Heals said to me on the bus on the way home tonight that he reckons we're ready now for the serious business. I think so too. That's what we're here for. One more day . . . and then it's on.

MARCH 7

Another day off, and I think we've all had enough of those. We're ready to go. I had a morning commitment at a conference to meet Hanumant Singh, the referee for the one-day tournament. It only lasted about half an hour, a friendly meeting with no drama. Both sides were in agreement. We want to play the game the best way — just get on with it and let the better side win.

Back at the resort I received a very pleasant surprise, and a gift I will cherish. Sir Garfield Sobers presented me with two prints that had been done of him — one of him batting, one bowling. They're slightly abstract in style, but very good and I'm proud and delighted to have them. They will sit nicely in the Taylor house! It was an unexpected gesture, and maybe one of the nice things that can happen to you when you're lucky enough to be team captain.

A swim, lunch with Steve Waugh and a light training session wrapped up this final day of 'getting ready'. Simmo and I were in agreement about training — that it should be pretty light; we didn't want to do too much the afternoon before the first one-dayer. We restricted it to a brief net session, just a bat and a bowl — no fielding. I hit the ball quite well, which was encouraging after the way I had scratched around yesterday. Obviously I want to play well in this series. It's not *essential* for the captain to do well, but it certainly helps. It's good for me, and it's good for the team. In my first couple of series as captain I have tried to be very positive with my batting and I'll be doing exactly the same here. I don't plan to change my thought processes or my approach just because we're playing the West Indies. Our aim is to be positive — to play the way we would against any opposition in the world. It's up to me to set the example. The weather remains warm. We need to save our energy — for tomorrow.

The decision has been made that we will be leaving out Ricky Ponting, Justin Langer and Damien Fleming. We haven't named our twelfth man yet — but it will probably be Glenn McGrath. We're playing on the same wicket that was used for last Sunday's game. It's a bit dry and hopefully will turn a bit, so the inclination is to take in two spinners.

Dinner at the Cafe Sol tonight, a Mexican meal, then an early night. The one-day games over here start at 9.30 a.m., so we are booked to leave the hotel at 7.30, figuring that it may take forty-five minutes or so to get to the ground. It's a school holiday in Barbados tomorrow, because of the cricket. The game is pretty close to a religion here, and it's a buzz to talk to the locals and to tap into the enthusiasm. Our cab driver tonight told me, 'Look, man, I want the West Indies to win, but I want some good cricket. Man, that's the main thing.'

I have a feeling deep down that it's going to be a great series. I hope so. After all it has been billed as the 'World Championship' and such a tag brings with it high expectations. My hope is that we can live up to them.

Chapter 2

THE ONE-DAYERS

MARCH 8

I'm back in my room — and we lost. But I wouldn't call it a disappointing loss. We failed by just six runs, chasing 257. My only real disappointment is that we let them score fifteen, maybe twenty runs more than they should have. For just about the first time our spinners let us down. It wasn't a great day for either Tim May or Shane Warne after the sort of contribution they have both made to the Australian cause this year. They went for 92 between them in fifteen overs. Most disappointing of all was that it happened on a wicket that was turning — and that at least to me is a great sign for the Test match ahead. I think we got a little carried away today — especially Warnie . . .

He bowled well in his first couple of overs, and got Phil Simmons with a beauty — a ball that bounced and turned, took the edge and came to me at slip. The ball was only sixteen or seventeen overs old then, so it was an encouraging sign for us. But I think then we got a bit carried away — especially Shane. He bowled a lot of different balls today. He tried to bowl his flipper and his wrong 'un . . . but they weren't coming out well and he got hit around. It's something we can certainly work on. He's bowling well. On these flatter wickets he's going to have to stay patient.

The thing is if we'd kept them down to 235 we would have won easily — because we batted very well. Everyone made some runs. Slats got 20-odd, I made 41, Boonie 85 not out, Mark Waugh 20-odd. We chased the target well and my impression was that their bowling lacked the sharpness or the quickness it usually has over here. I'll qualify that by adding 'at this stage'. I've seen blokes like Curtly Ambrose go through the motions in a game or two — and then a week later be bowling like demons. I won't read too much into it, but at the moment he is certainly not anywhere near the sort of pace I know he can muster. Courtney Walsh bowled reasonably well, without bowling all that sharp.

I don't like losing cricket matches at any time. But I think there was a lot of good came out of today. We need to cross the t's and dot the i's a bit more effectively — for example we bowled seven no-balls today — and when we do that we're going to be very competitive, and especially in the Test matches. From the batting point of view it's very important we keep challenging them. If they get half a sniff that they're getting on top, all of a sudden they're all over you. When we get it right I'm sure we've got the bowlers to win the Tests.

It's 11.30 p.m. now and I'm back from the Ship Inn. A group of us had a real good talk about the game tonight, about where we went wrong. I talked to Warnie about being a bit more patient with his bowling, and he agreed he needed to do that. If he remains patient in his approach I think he's going to have these guys in a lot of trouble. They don't play him too well.

We were on the receiving end of some cab-driver wisdom tonight. The bloke who brought us back to the hotel said to me when we got in, 'Hey, man — you guys going to win the first Test?'

We told him we aimed to.

'I hope so,' he said, 'because I've got my money on you.' I asked him why he'd backed us.

'Because everyone else is betting against you,' he said. Then he offered some advice: 'You don't want to be scared of these guys. They're not that good.'

Funny thing, the cabby had tapped into *exactly* the way we were approaching things.

And so to bed. An interesting start to the tour. The last time here we started with a win, and went home losers. Maybe it's going to work the other way . . .

MARCH 9

Today was a travel day, and in the West Indies, they're tough. It's not like flying from Sydney to Brisbane. Every time you change islands you've got to go through Immigration, Customs and all that. We flew from Barbados to Trinidad, about thirty-five minutes in the air. Yet we left Barbados at two o'clock and didn't reach our destination, the Trinidad Hilton, until seven o'clock at night. It's a hard slog for a short journey. We spent at least two hours in the VIP room at Trinidad Airport.

Trinidad is a different world to Barbados. It has a great deal of Indian culture, and food, whereas places such as Barbados and Antigua are more African-based. One of our liaison officers recommended an Indian restaurant called The Monsoon for dinner, and a group of us ate there. After the meal when we were out the front waiting for a cab, three or four beggars confronted us for money. It was something we hadn't experienced in Barbados and reminded us a little of India.

MARCH 10

We trained in the afternoon, which is not our preferred choice. But the West Indians like to train in the mornings (as we do) and today we had to settle for a two o'clock session. It was a fairly light workout. The weather is warm and humid, and the weekend shapes as a tough one — a double-header, with one-day games on both Saturday and Sunday.

Afterwards we had a couple of beers at a pub called the Pelican and I had a good chat to Shane Warne about what lies head. The press are really building this into a Lara versus Warne tour, and of course cricket is not about that at all. I have never played in a series in which one single player has been the winning factor — and it won't be this way this time either. We obviously want Warnie to do well — but the pressure's not as great on him as maybe he thinks it is. We talked about that today. I want him to relax and enjoy the tour — and not get caught up in all this media hype. After the Pelican we had a quick meal at McDonald's, but I would not like that to get back to our physio Errol Alcott. He wouldn't approve.

Tonight, a game of blackjack with a few of the guys. In bed by ten o'clock with the weekend much in mind. We're one-down, and we need to turn that around.

MARCH 11

Today the second one-day International at Port of Spain, Trinidad. And the victory we had hoped for. A game that went well all day for us. We won the toss, which is always a good thing over here. I equate it to being worth 10-20 runs as it is in Australia. We batted and made 260, a very good score and the product of a real 'team' effort. Slats got 55, I only made 16 — but hit the ball all right — a good 50 from Steve Waugh, and, at the end, a very, very helpful 50 from Ian Healy, off 45 balls, which pushed us up from a likely score of around 240 to 260.

The Healy contribution proved to be the difference in the game, because we got them all out for 234. They still had two overs to go, so were pretty much on target but we managed to get the wickets when we needed them. Brian Lara got 62 for them and played ominously well. He was in much better touch than his innings in Barbados, and this is not a good sign. Carl Hooper again played well and got 55. Those two are their form players — the men to watch.

I stopped the celebrations after the game. Our guys were obviously happy about winning, but frankly I was a little disappointed in our performance, especially in the field. We are below our best, lacking some urgency. I suppose it's understandable; we've had a long summer, but the truth of it is we've got to get sharp if we are going to win this series.

The lack of urgency in our approach showed in the fact that when the first drinks break came (after one hour) we had bowled only fifteen overs. It was unusual for us. Usually we hustle through the overs very quickly, keeping the pressure on the batsmen by bowling plenty of balls at them. Usually by the first drinks break we are up to seventeen or eighteen overs. We're languishing . . . a bit slow . . . and I mentioned it to the blokes after the win. I reckon that's the best time for a captain to express any reservations he has about a performance. Everyone's happy and positive, and they'll take it on board. I just told them I believed there was improvement in the side — and that we *had* to make improvement if we were going to be the best side this summer.

The first two games have been outstanding contests — great value for the fans. My concerns are in only two areas — the fielding . . . and Shane Warne. Again today it was very apparent that he is not bowling at his best at the moment. He has been a class act for us in recent years, a match winner many times. But he's in a bit of a trough here just at present and today he again 'went funny'. He bowled 10 overs and took one for 63, and the West Indians are really going after him, which I suppose we knew they were always going to do. Warnie's problem at the moment is that he's dropping short, and paying the penalty. Usually if he errs, he errs on the full side, which is the best way for a leg spinner to be. A short ball from a leg spinner generally goes for 4, and that's the way it was today on too many occasions. We've got three or four weeks to the first Test, so there is time enough to get it right.

MARCH 12

It's 9.50 on Sunday night — and I'm sitting here hoping that today will be about as bad as it gets on this tour. The third one-dayer was a pretty ordinary game all round for us, with some really bad news at the end of it. On the third ball of Damien Fleming's second spell, he suddenly clutched the shoulder that has troubled him throughout the season. It was the end of his contribution to the match — and the news tonight after consultation with Errol Alcott is that Damien won't be taking any more part in the tour, and will be flying home as soon as he can. It was one of those days.

We started off by losing the toss. We went in without Craig McDermott and Mark Waugh — both of them have niggling injuries, and it was a chance to give Damien Fleming and Ricky Ponting a chance. They both actually did well; Ricky made 40-odd and Damien had 1-18 off his first seven-over spell, until disaster struck. He troubled both openers, and Hooper and Lara too — the two West Indies form players of the moment. For quite a time things were going nicely. We had them two for 26 off about nine overs, but they finished up with 5-282. We got absolutely hammered by Brian Lara, who made 139 off about 120 balls. He just smashed us around and turned what would have been a 230 score into 282. If he was to have a good day I would prefer it was today rather than one of the Test matches. The 283 target was always going to be pretty tough to get.

On the bowling front it was a real bad day all round, what with Damien's tragic news and Warnie getting some stick again. He finished with 0-52 and continues to bowl below his best — although the fact is the West Indians are playing very well. They are backing themselves as only the West Indies can, and hitting him hard and often.

On the batting side of things we had a disastrous start. Slats and I both got run out from direct hits. I was hitting the ball pretty well actually when, on 26, Carl Hooper got me with an arrow-straight throw. It set the scene for the rest of the day. We got to three for 100-odd and looked all right, but then another run-out, a freakish catch and we were on the slide. Next thing we were all out for 140-odd. The margin was not a major worry. If you're going to lose a one-day game, you might as well lose by 130 as by five or ten. It was just a disastrous day. We lost the toss, struck a wicket that was wearing, playing low and slow, and we got a towelling. Life goes on.

Tonight the downhill path continued. The hotel has lost my bloody laundry and a huge search is underway. We're due to move on at 5.30 in the morning, and I can only hope they'll track it down and send it on. Things aren't exactly going our way. We've got two days to get it back together in St Vincent before our next match . . .

MARCH 13

A 4.30 a.m. wake-up, and thanks to an on-time Liat eight-seater (Leeward Island Air Travel — or perhaps more aptly 'Leave Island Anytime') we were over to St Vincent in the Windward Islands bright and early. After the Great Laundry Search last night, I'm in further trouble. My 'coffin' (cricket bag) arrived safely but not the rest of my luggage. As we took off we saw some of our bags sitting forlornly on the tarmac. Fingers are crossed.

This afternoon we repeated a magical experience of the last tour here, and took a boat cruise which involved some snorkelling. Only Michael Slater and Glenn McGrath missed out through a 'communications glitch' and it was a damned shame. It was a terrific day, just as it had been last tour. We had a swim under a waterfall in a beautiful spot, and then did some snorkelling, checking out the marine life in beautiful clear waters. The blokes captaining our two boats — Carly and Big Gully — then pulled out an esky which contained some extra-strong rum punch. The first taste was pretty ordinary, a bit rough . . . but it got better. The afternoon sort of drifted on to the point where we were back late, but happy, then met the guys from the other boat in a bar where the rum punch was favourite again. It was a really good day — just what we needed after yesterday. And I was really wrapped about how much positive cricket talk there was about how we could improve, what we should avoid in future, how things were going to be better. It was just one of those days that I'm sure we'll all remember long after the tour is over.

MARCH 14

Today I had a call at ten to seven in the morning — from a fan wanting a ticket! Just what I needed. Rudely awakened, I took the opportunity to ring my wife Judi for a chat. She's in good spirits. Then to training at Victoria Grounds. The nets are pretty ordinary here so we decided to have some different drills and make it a competitive sort of session. It was good and I think everyone enjoyed it. We were out there for a couple of hours, but a lot of it was in setting up things, so we didn't do too much in the heat.

Tomorrow we face the game we need to win to stay in the one-day tournament. Tonight, something different and special — a meal organised down on the beach by our men from the boat cruise, Carly and Big Gully, cooked by a mate of theirs named Scarborough. It was a local speciality, a sort of fish stew with vegetables, and it was absolutely magnificent. All the guys from the dive shop with whom we have become pally came along, and it was a really enjoyable night, just standing there on the beach eating this wonderful food. Scarborough is going to write down the recipe for Steve Waugh, and I'll grab a copy of it too. Fingers are crossed all-round for tomorrow. It would be nice to win that one and slide the series into a fifth-match decider. With the pressure on then, I think we could do the job.

MARCH 15

I'm just back from the ground — and we lost again. To be very honest I'm not too worried about that, although it's always better to win and to be 3-1 down doesn't sit too well. What I am a good deal more worried about is the fact that we're not playing well. I said at the start that I believed we had the talent to win over here, and I'm still sure of that. But the thing about contests in the West Indies is that it takes *more than* talent to win. Right at this moment we have some deficiencies, and we're going to have to turn it around pretty quickly. At the moment we haven't mustered the toughness or the application to win over here.

Specifically the batsmen aren't making the big scores that we need. The aim of all of us once we get a start against them is to go on and make a score. Today, again, it didn't happen. I went early, for 3, and no excuses there. Mark Waugh was going well, but got to 26 and got out. After thirty overs we were 2-130 on a wicket which had some bounce in it. We were heading for a score of 250 or so. Then Keith Arthurton, a left-arm orthodox spinner but only a part-timer, got Michael Slater and David Boon out, and suddenly we were 4-137. We scratched our way up to 9-210, forty or so short of what we should have been. Our need is for someone to make a good score. Most of us are making the 20s, 30s and 40s, but we need someone to build the foundation of a big innings and at the moment that's just not happening.

Rain reduced their target to 206 in 46 overs although it took them only 43.1 overs to claim victory with the loss of three wickets. On the positive side of the ledger there was some improvement in the way we bowled. But not enough to control them the way we'd like to. They are still attacking furiously and hitting us around at will. Craig McDermott has a shoulder injury and is not bowling at top pace at the moment, which is a definite worry.

The one good thing that came out of the day was the way that Shane Warne lifted. He bowled a hell of a lot better took 2-33 off 9.1 overs and bowled some beautiful stuff.

The fielding, though, continues to lack urgency. Maybe it's just the fact that we've played a heap of one-day cricket this year. The count is somewhere up around twenty-five matches and perhaps we're just a bit stale in the way we are approaching the one-day game. I know I feel that way and I am really looking forward to some first-class cricket — and especially the Test matches that lie ahead.

We need to be up a notch — to be fresher, to be enjoying it more. There was a crucial stage again today when we were bowling and we had them under some pressure. Yet each time that has happened they seem to be able to lash out, hit our quick men back over the top and break any sort of tightening grip we may have had. The fact that they are doing that — hitting our quicks high and straight over their heads — suggests to me that they are in the frame of mind to do what they like with us just at the moment. That has to be a worry.

One good thing is that I honestly believe the adjustments we need are only in small areas. We certainly have to lift our energy level, to come to terms with the fact that we are not playing England or New Zealand — we are playing the West Indies, who have that enormously proud tradition at home. They are undefeated in the last fifteen years in a Test series. They are not going to give *that* away easily. If we don't lift, we're not going to win. We have to up the ante, and it has to happen very soon. From my point of view the sooner the one-day stuff is out of the way, the better. We've got to get stuck into some hard cricket — see the bowlers bowling under first-class conditions and the batsman batting under first-class conditions, and making some scores. We need application, we need concentration. And if it doesn't start to happen very shortly we won't be winners here — and that would be a crying shame, because this Australian team has the talent to do it.

MARCH 16

There was a good deal of early fumbling today as we took the next leg of the long haul. The Liat flight to Guyana via Trinidad was late off the ground, and what's more there wasn't enough room on board for (a) all our luggage and (b) Shane Warne, Ian Healy and Mike Walsh, our scorer. Our pilot and hostess assured me there was a chartered flight leaving fifteen minutes after ours that would bring them safely across. But when the flight to Guyana was due to leave Trinidad airport, the trio still hadn't arrived. The rest of us took the flight anyway and made it to our hotel in Georgetown in Guyana by about two o'clock in the afternoon. On arrival we found that we only had fourteen of the sixty-one pieces of luggage we had booked on at St Vincent. Heals, Warnie and Walshy spent six hours in Trinidad before making it across, so they weren't too delighted with the whole thing.

This was not a great day. At the hotel there was no room for me — I wasn't on the list. I had to get across the point that I was captain of the Australian cricket team, and would they please find me a room. Finally they found me one which turned out to be an unmade-up mess. At least I did better than some of the boys. Craig McDermott's room had no beds, and in some of the others there were blokes renovating and plastering. Back downstairs at the desk there was a great deal of reorganising and shuffling before we all finally got settled in.

This afternoon in my room I had a big talk with all the batsmen. We talked about the West Indies bowling and how it seemed that all of us were comfortable with them, which was unusual, but that we were not taking advantage of it. It was a good session. We chatted about a lot of team things, about the need to build team harmony and get together more as a unit. It was really good stuff, perhaps one of those moments on a tour when you feel a small but significant *switch*. Tomorrow the bowlers are coming in for a similar chat.

Back at the hotel Warnie and Heals and Walshy have finally arrived, and Heals is not happy. I can understand that. I can imagine the reaction if we left three or four of the West Indians posted somewhere in Australia on one of their tours. But we've got to live with these things. At our first team meeting here we talked about the problems we would (probably) run into with travel and baggage and accommodation, and that we had to rise above all that and keep the whingeing down to a minimum. Today we'll be making our disappointment known — three team members left behind, and baggage still who-knows-where. It's not good enough, but we've got to get on.

In the local Guyana paper I am on the receiving end of something of a bagging from Tony Cosier. I took in what he had to say. Tony is a very nice bloke, and a very good commentator. He was very critical of me taking off Shane Warne at the time I did in yesterday's match. In one sense he was correct, because we were doing okay when Shane was at the crease. But when I go back over my tactics I'm still quite happy with them. The bottom line is that we had forty-six overs to bowl — that's ten overs each from my specialist bowlers McDermott, McGrath, Warne, plus I had to get six overs out of a fifth bowler — who turned out to be a combination of David Boon and Greg Blewett. While the Windies were down, just after Shane had taken a wicket I figured it would be a good chance to try and sneak in those six overs. Unfortunately it didn't work. They got away from us, and we couldn't pull them back. Warnie came back on and bowled well in his second spell, but even then we couldn't get back on top. It was the sort of punt a captain has to take in a cricket match now and then.

It's always an easy game from the outside, and it's disappointing at times to read some of the criticism from experts outside the fence. Too often it seems they go for the negative and criticise, without perhaps probing deeply enough as to why you may have done something. Criticism, and strong criticism, of course makes livelier reading — and I understand that. Tony Cosier knew that I had to get six overs out of my fifth bowler at some stage. If I had left those six overs to the end things may have been different . . . and they may not have been. I did what I did and I'd do exactly the same tomorrow. As a captain you've got to analyse your own game all the time and follow your gut instincts. You make your decision . . . and then you live with it.

MARCH 17

The nightmare continues. It's 1.20 on Friday afternoon and our missing gear from St Vincent still hasn't arrived. The lost load includes all the 'coffins' containing our cricket gear. We had left them all at the St Vincent ground at 5 o'clock last Wednesday afternoon, where we were promised they would be flown straight to Trinidad and then on to Georgetown. Word has just arrived that they are finally at the airport, and now on their way. If they're not, we can forget about this afternoon's planned practice session. Our team manager Jack Edwards, Bob Simpson and I have had a chat with the West Indies Cricket Board's chief executive officer Steve Camach about the mess-up, and hopefully things will improve. Touring is never easy, but it should be a hell of a lot easier than it has been these past few days.

This morning I talked with our bowlers, a chat similar to the one I had with the batsmen yesterday, about lifting our level of intensity and concentration, especially at critical times. It was a fruitful session with a lot of feedback from them. I appreciated that. I get sick of hearing myself talking . . . and I'm sure they get sick of it too.

The press clippings arrived from Australia today, covering the things I had to say after the game in St Vincent. They're a mixture, but most of them are pretty close to the mark. But I'm going to have a word with Robert Craddock (Sydney *Telegraph Mirror*). I did make the point to the media about my belief that we are one-day cricket stale at the moment, but that our achievements on this tour would be remembered for what we managed in the Test matches, and they were what we were really looking forward to. But certain members of the press — and especially Craddock — have read into my statements the doubt (from me) that we can win over here. I didn't say that. I *did* say that our intensity levels were low and our cricket not good enough . . . at the moment. I was talking one-day cricket, but Craddock has taken a quantum leap to the conclusion that we can't win over here. The fact is I believe we have a *very good* chance of winning over here. His article was negative and disappointing. It also wasn't accurate, and I plan to have a quiet word with him.

It's now 10 o'clock, the night before the final one-day game. It's been a full day, and a good one. I was really happy with the discussions I had with the bowlers. And my talk with Craddock (whose nickname is 'Crash') was positive too. I told the journos earlier in the season that I would keep the lines of communication open, and that I would always make the point if I felt they had taken something I had said (or done) the wrong way. Crash was very good. What he had written, he said, he believed was correct. He appreciated my pointing out that his interpretation was not mine, and that I believed he had erred. There are certainly no hard feelings. In no way do I want the press to write just what *I* might want them to write. Their job is to write the truth, to tell people back home exactly what is going on. If that truth happens to be personally painful to me or the team, well, so be it.

Tomorrow, a game of considerable interest, for various reasons. Craig McDermott is out. His shoulder is troubling him greatly, and there's no way he can bowl at top pace. At this stage of the tour it's certainly not worth risking him. We'll probably give Shane Warne a spell too, so as to freshen him for what lies ahead. We are keen to get Tim May back in, and there's a chance we may even use Brendon Julian even though he's only just arrived after forty hours on the plane to replace Damien Fleming and is probably the worse for wear. We'll check him out in the morning. I'm positive about the outcome of the separate meetings with the batsmen and bowlers. There is one theory that we've been 'individualising' too much, thinking about everything on a personal basis rather than focusing on the tour as a team situation. At the end of it people will be talking about how we went as a *team*, not how we went as individuals. We've got a drought to break on this tour — and the only way we're going to do it is by working together harmoniously and single-mindedly as a cricket *team*. That's the way we're going to approach these next six or seven weeks.

MARCH 18

The news is no better. The clock has just ticked over from midnight on Saturday, and I'm going to bed a losing Australian captain again. A disappointing day — another loss, in the fifth one-dayer. Today we did just about everything right at the Bourda Ground in Georgetown . . . except win the match. We won the toss and batted, in very hot conditions. Michael Slater and I put on about 80 for the first wicket, and I went on to get 66, which was pleasing.

I batted okay, but without hitting my drives the way I'd like to. Today I had hoped to set the standard after all the discussions about us batsmen making big scores once we had got a start and I was disappointed to hole out on the boundary, just when I should have been ramming home our advantage. In all truthfulness I just got tired. It was tremendously, crushingly hot. Mark Waugh stayed to make a great 70 and then was unfortunately run out. Mark was in the middle of a real bad time, just when things were looking great. We were 2-203 and then Steve Waugh, Ricky Ponting and Mark all went within the space of two runs. We still made 286 off our fifty overs, but on a very small ground with a flat wicket. Still, 286 was defendable.

The fact was, we didn't bowl well enough today. We bowled far too full — a lot of half-volleys — and we got punished for it. Phil Simmons made 70 runs off about sixty balls and really smashed us. Carl Hooper made another 50, and he's looking like the one. Carl's record against us in Test cricket is not great, but this time he's looking a different player. He's more positive, backing himself — hitting the boundaries when he wants to hit the boundaries. He's a threat in the Tests, no doubt.

The bottom line was that they made five for 287, getting the runs with two and a half overs to spare. They were really too good for us today. Admittedly we had Craig McDermott and Shane Warne out, our two best bowlers, but we had enough runs up on the board to really stretch them, and we couldn't do it. They had 104 runs after fifteen overs. They really smashed us.

The question we have to answer is: are we going to be good enough in what lies ahead to keep the pressure on these guys, and bowl them out? That is the sixty-four dollar question. Our batting was okay. We lacked the one really big score that we are searching for, even though all the guys looked reasonably comfortable against their bowling.

There is a great deal of irony in the current situation of the tour. At this stage four years ago we'd just won the one-dayers 4-1. The last one that tour had also been in Guyana and we had chased a big score — and got it to win the match. Everyone was saying how good we were and what a great chance we were to knock them off in the Tests. But when it came to crunch time we were nowhere near good enough. We slid behind 2-nil, though we ended up losing only 2-1 by winning the final Test. This time, the situation is exactly reversed. The one-day scorecard reads 4-1, but the other way. Is it an omen?

We've got thirteen days to get it right. Thirteen days to the first Test. Thirteen days to get the mix right of what is a team of exceptional talent. We can't afford to lose that first Test match. A win or a draw, and we're in with a great chance of taking the series. But a loss there would make it very tough indeed. Words like desire, hunger, application, determination are going to have to be much in our minds these next two weeks. We're improving, but we have more to do.

BEN RADFORD/ALLSPORT•AUSTRALIAN PICTURE LIBRARY

Carl Hooper seen here in the fourth one-day international at St Vincent. Hooper's contribution in this 5 match series was 84, 55, 41, 60 not out and 50. With 290 runs at 72.5 average, he was one of the main reasons the Windies won 4-1. He could not reproduce this form in the test series under much greater pressure.

Chapter 3

THE
BUILD-UP

MARCH 19

A day off in Georgetown, which, frankly, is not a great place to have a day off in. It's a Sunday and a public holiday as well because of a Hindu festival, so just about everything is closed. I've taken the chance to do some work on the book, and a bit of lazing around the pool, too.

Tomorrow we play Guyana, and I wonder what that will bring. We're leaving out Steve Waugh, David Boon and Paul Reiffel who are all in pretty good form, plus Craig, who is still wrestling with his shoulder problem. I don't think Guyana are a terribly strong side, and Carl Hooper won't be playing. He's gone back to London to organise some business to do with his County side, Kent. Whether it's an important game for them or not, it's up to us to get the most out of it. We're the ones who have to start turning things around. We've lost the one-day series and we've done plenty of talking about what we *should* be doing, and what we have to do. But talk's cheap. It's time for some action. It was a good day to think about all that, a quiet and reflective day in Georgetown.

MARCH 20

Today, disaster struck the team. And not on the cricket field, but on a road which leads back to our hotel. I'll talk about the cricket shortly. What happened was this. At the end of the day's play a group of us ran back from the ground to the hotel — Craig McDermott, David Boon, Erroll Alcott and I. As usual Craig was way out in front. He's quicker than the rest of us. I was about a minute behind, with the other two a minute or so back behind me. All of a sudden I 'lost' Billy . . . and then I caught up to him. He was up against a wall, screaming in agony and crying. He'd gone over on an ankle, and badly. I've never seen an ankle swell up so quickly. It was like a balloon. We had to get a cab to bring him back to the hotel, as there was no way he could walk. We packed his leg in ice, and if the ankle wasn't broken it was obvious that he'd torn something very badly. Billy was in bad trouble, and so were we. It's amazing. Damien Fleming is already home, and now it looks like Craig McDermott's tour is over as well. We've lost the one-dayers and now we've lost our two front-line bowlers. It's not looking great.

Craig's accident came after a day which had been a good one for us. We lost the toss on a flat wicket with absolutely no grass on it, and bowled them out for 105. Glenn McGrath got five for 40-odd and Brendon Julian bowled well for 2-23. We didn't start too well. Slats got 2 and I managed only 4, but things improved. Mark Waugh hammered 75 off sixty-five balls and Greg Blewett is 82 not out. We walked off in good spirits. Half an hour later we were in terrible trouble.

I'm not too pessimistic. I look back to Pakistan, my first series as captain and to the first Test in which we were missing both McDermott and Fleming. Under difficulties we played a great Test match. We lost it by a wicket — but we should have won. Adversity often brings out the best in people, and that's the line we'll be pushing hard after today's misfortune.

Tonight at a place called Del Casa a group of us wrestled with the events of today. Simmo was there and Babsie (David Boon), Heals, Maysie and me. We'd seen Craig at the hotel when he came back from the doctor before we headed out. The good news is that he has no break in the ankle. But that's all the good news. The rest of the news is bad enough — that he has a torn ligament and a ruptured capsule. It's about as bad as it can get. We haven't made the final decision yet about what to do with Craig, but I'm thinking that there's not much option but for him to go home. It's the way we're all thinking . . . Craig too. He's on crutches, and maybe he'll be walking within the week. But we don't have the luxury of much time, and he's got to be bowling within three weeks for us to even consider playing him in the last two Tests.

Craig McDermott – his tour was sadly cut short due to injury.

BEN RADFORD/ALLSPORT•AUSTRALIAN PICTURE LIBRARY

That's what we talked about tonight — that our two opening bowlers in the last Test match we played (McDermott and Fleming) are *both* now almost certainly gone. But we talked about opportunity too — about the opportunity presented to Paul Reiffel, Glenn McGrath and Brendon Julian by what has happened. They've all been around long enough to put their hands up to be counted. In adversity, the chance is with them. To win the series we've got to bowl the Windies out. If we can't bowl them out, we can't win.

MARCH 21

Today, thankfully, was a pretty quiet one compared with yesterday's dramas. We kicked on against Guyana and made 373 in reply to their 105, with Greg Blewett advancing to 116, Justin Langer toughing it out for 55 — an innings in which he didn't look too impressive but, to his credit, hung on well — Heals getting 29, and Warnie and Tim May chipping in at the end. At stumps we had them 6-165, with Brendon Julian turning in good figures of 4-40 even though his performance could be deemed a little *strange*. He mixed up a bunch of no-balls with some ordinary balls — and wickets off very good balls. The good news is that he is taking wickets. It's official now that Craig is going home, leaving Barbados on Friday night bound for Brisbane and some rehabilitation. Wickets are what we need, and Brendon came up with some today.

The press quizzed me pretty strongly about Craig's misfortune, and what we would be doing to plug the gap. I told them exactly what I thought: that we must get a guy over here who's in form, and that with the Sheffield Shield final to be played in Australia at the weekend it could logically be a 'bowl off' with the prize of a trip going to the quick who did best. Whoever comes over is only going to have a possibility of playing the last two Tests. We need someone who'd get stuck into it as soon as he gets here, someone who's smack-bang ready to go.

It was a good day for us, a welcome respite after a bit of a rough trot lately. There's been some talk in the papers about the bribery allegations in Pakistan and a few of the guys are obviously concerned about that. Hopefully it won't affect their cricket, but it's only human nature that it will play on their minds to some extent because it's a nasty business. It's up to me to make sure they are switched on to cricket and the job at hand.

An interesting meal tonight at the Palm Court with Steve and Mark Waugh, Michael Slater, Justin Langer and a guy known as Big Daddy, who is something of a wheeler around here. He's a Rasterman and he pulls quite a bit of weight in Georgetown. It's amazing when you sit at dinner with a guy like Big Daddy just how quick the service is and how much attention is paid to your table. I enjoyed the night.

MARCH 22

We finished off Guyana in about an hour this morning, bundling them out for 207, to win by an innings and 61 runs. It wasn't really any sort of great practice session for us, but it was good to win, and some useful things came out of it. Brendon Julian finished with 5-54 off eleven overs, a mixture of good and bad as I said. Glenn McGrath got two more to add to his bag of five wickets in the first innings, and he's going well. And Warnie got a couple of wickets this morning with his flipper, a really good sign for us because that particular ball hasn't been coming out very well at all for the last four or five months. He bowled one and got another LBW, so that was good stuff for us.

The game was over by about 11 o'clock and back at the hotel we lazed around for a bit before starting to get ready for some more island-hopping. We'll be at the airport at 4.30 p.m. and back at our hotel base in Barbados at 11 p.m. Six and a half hours from hotel to hotel, another solid haul.

MARCH 23

Today started out in Barbados, before a midday departure to St Lucia, about 200 kilometres away. We were met by a steel band, before heading to a very nice hotel on what looks to be a lovely island. It's a popular holiday resort spot, which is probably not what we need at the moment. The game here starts on Saturday and should be a good tough one, which is what we *need*. They've picked pretty close to their Second XI Test side, including some ex-Test players, and some blokes who are angling for spots in the top line-up. It was a good day. A convivial meal tonight with Simmo, Jack Edwards, Errol Alcott and Mike Walsh then back to the hotel to be greeted by a couple of faxes — one from my manager John Fordham and one from Mum and Dad. It was nice to have that link with back home. My dad Tony didn't say too much in his contribution — about three lines — but he came out with something pretty wise in talking about Craig McDermott's departure from the team. He wrote: 'If you can't out-gun them you're going to have to out-general them.' It was typical of my old man — short and sharp and right on the money. I'm really looking forward to this game: it's a chance for some individual and collective toughening up in the team, and we need that. The business end of the tour is just about to start and we've got to get cracking.

MARCH 24

The Friday before the game — and it's looking more and more like a day off. It teemed all night and I woke this morning to the sound of the rain still tumbling down. We're going to try and do something later this afternoon, but I doubt it will be anything to do with cricket because the ground all around is absolutely saturated. It's disappointing really. We were all looking forward to a practice session today, and to the game. But if it rains, it rains, and we cricketers can't do much about that.

The skies finally cleared about two o'clock this afternoon and gave us the chance to do a few things down at the beach — a game of volleyball and touch rugby league. The get-together also gave me the chance to have a talk to the guys and give them a rocket about their attitude. I don't think it's good enough at the moment. Everyone is getting on very well and the team spirit is good, but our attitude at game time has been the problem. Today I asked each one of them for an increased effort — starting tomorrow. Whether we're going to get any cricket, I don't know. It's still very wet underfoot.

MARCH 25

As I had predicted, no play today. The day itself wasn't too bad — a short, sharp shower in the morning, then clearing. But when we got to the ground it was still pretty much under water. The wicket was covered, but there was a large damp patch at one end. It wasn't a tough decision to make. At eleven o'clock, play was off for the day. By then the sun was out, and hopes are rising that we'll get a start tomorrow. What should have been a day of tough cricket turned into a bit of a holiday with some wind-surfing and swimming and just general relaxing around the hotel. Given fair weather we've got three days of cricket left in this game, and we need them.

Tonight I caught up with some old school friends for dinner at a seafood restaurant across the way, which didn't have the world's best food but not the world's worst either. A pleasant night and an early one, ready for some cricket tomorrow.

MARCH 26

The good weather has come back, and today was a pretty fair one for Oz. We arrived to find the ground in reasonable condition, but I promptly lost the toss. Fortunately they sent us in. Phew! I was going to bat anyway, so it turned out to be a Clayton's toss. At the end of a lively day we were 5-322 off only eighty-three overs. I missed out unfortunately — made only three and out in a very similar way to the way I lost my wicket in Guyana — caught at first slip trying to drive off the back foot. It's disappointing. I'm seeing the ball quite well, and feeling solid. I'm just being a bit impatient I think — trying to force the pace too soon. It's what I want to be doing; I want to be seen to be doing the positive stuff out there and I feel as if I'm playing well enough to do it. Today I was out trying to play a back-foot drive. The ball took the edge and I was caught at slip. Slats got dropped off an easy chance on 30, then went on to make an excellent 90. He played very well. Mark Waugh ran himself out on 73 after playing superbly and Steve Waugh is 73 not out. By the end Heals had made 42 not out.

There were some really good signs for us against what effectively was their second-string Test attack. They had Ian Bishop, a guy named Cuffy who toured with the last West Indian team to India and played Test cricket, Anderson Cummins, a Test player, and the leg-spinner Dhanraj who is in the Test squad for next week. So their bowling attack was quite solid. Despite that we dominated just about all day, and it was a day to give us all heart. The rain came back near the end and I'm not sure what sort of shape the ground will be in tomorrow, because we want the chance to bowl at them. I'm going to declare on the overnight score so we can get some bowling practice. From my point of view there was some personal disappointment today, but well balanced by my pleasure at the way we played.

MARCH 27

A tardy start, thanks to some early morning rain. We lost an hour and a half's play at the start of the day, and at lunch had them 1-23. We came out after lunch and with Brendon Julian bowling particularly well had them 4-70 at one stage. After that things didn't go too well. We got a wicket late in the day but at stumps they were five for 260-odd. Warnie was a bit of a mixture. He ended up with 2-84 off fourteen overs, bowling well in his first spell, but not so well in his second. It was a bit of a disappointing day. It would have been good to knock them over for 200 or so and have another bat. In a way it followed the pattern of the tour so far — an encouraging day followed by a not-so-encouraging one. As regards a preparation for a Test match . . . well, I'm not really sure. There were good signs and bad signs. I went to bed tonight with the sound of rain bucketing down on the hotel roof.

MARCH 28

Early this morning I took a phone call from their captain Roland Holder who reported that the ground was under water. We headed down there. It was quickly apparent there was no chance of further play, so the 'game abandoned' sign went up, and that was that. By 11 a.m. I was back in my room, packing for Barbados, with the plan being that some of us will head across tonight rather than in the morning. It would be good if we could *all* go tonight of course, but as you may have already gathered, travel in the West Indies is not the easiest part of the operation. The rest of the boys will come over in the morning.

A lost day, to some extent. I had a yarn with the press guys and the main theme was our enthusiasm for the Tests and how we just wanted to get on to them. Let the battle begin.

MARCH 29

Afternoon training today, once the second planeload of the team had arrived from St Lucia. I was a bit scratchy and I suppose it's not surprising. My last two innings have been fairly brief affairs, 4 and 3. I'd been hitting the ball well, though, and I don't think I'm too much out of form. But it would have been good to get some more batting in that last match. It's been more than a week now since I spent any time in the middle. Towards the end of the net I was starting to hit them okay. I'm looking forward to tomorrow's session.

Back at the hotel we had a team meeting at six o'clock, and it was very encouraging. The emphasis was on the fact that we had five weeks to go — and it would be what happened during those five weeks that everyone would remember from the tour. No-one would remember the one-day games, or the match against Guyana or the President's XI. The tour is about the four Test matches that lie ahead. I said to the guys today, let's put everything we can into these five weeks. If we do that, hopefully we'll get something out of it. Hopefully that 'something' will be a series win. All we can do as players — and all I can do as captain — is give it our best shot. If we do that, I'll be proud and happy. It was a terrific meeting. There was a lot of talk, a lot of input from all the guys. I like that. I have always felt that team meetings were for the 'team' — not just for blokes to sit there listening to the captain or coach rattling on.

Tonight we had our team dinner down at Acra Beach at a place owned by our hotel. It was a good meal, and a good night. We just sat there chatting, talking cricket, until about 9.30 p.m.

This was a good day. The Test match is only thirty-six hours away now, and the signs are encouraging. Spirits are buoyant and I sense we are pretty close to ready.

Steve Waugh, a man with a passion for cricket's history, at Sir Frank Worrell's memorial.

MARCH 30

It's Test eve, 8.37 p.m. to be exact, and I'm just back from dinner with David Boon, Mike Walsh and Jack Edwards. Two beers before dinner, a meal — and now I'm back for some reading, and some thinking. I hope I can tire myself enough to get some sleep! The place is buzzing, and I'm talking about our team. The intensity level in all areas has lifted amazingly these last couple of days, and there is an air of excitement about the guys which is just great. Of course only time will answer the question whether we're good enough to do what we came to do, but honestly I can't ask for much more than the way things are at the moment.

Today I had a very good net session, just what I needed. I hit the ball well, dragged back some confidence and played some good shots. The way I'm feeling is pretty hard to put into words. There's excitement, some apprehension and a mixture of a few other things. Mainly I'm looking forward to getting down to business. It's funny, you know. We've been over here for four weeks or so, yet there's a strange feeling that we've really achieved nothing, done nothing. The one-dayers could have been better for us, but really the way I feel tonight, they were just like ships that passed by and were gone, leaving no great impression. Our main destination is now, in the arena of the Tests.

It's now 7 a.m. A few final thoughts as the day begins. As I had feared, I had a pretty ordinary night's sleep. It was the same way before the first Tests against England and Pakistan. I read until about ten and then was drifting off when there was a knock at the door with a message about someone chasing tickets. They're always asking for tickets over here. So, I was awake until about midnight, woke at 4 a.m., woke again at six — and I've been just lying here half-dozing. Now it's time to get up and go and play Test cricket.

Chapter 4

FIRST TEST, BARBADOS

MARCH 31

First day, first Test — and the news is good. I lost the toss, which was not a great start, and they decided to bat. That would have been my choice, too. But it was a deceptive wicket, one that did a bit more than either Richie Richardson or I expected. It had some bounce and some life and early on we had them three for 6! I was thinking, 'Wow! what's going on here!' But Hooper and Lara got together and by lunch they were heading out of the woods at 3-116. To the credit of our blokes we bowled tighter and better again after lunch. Carl Hooper went, and that started a procession.

Immediately after Hooper's dismissal we got rid of the danger man, Brian Lara, caught in the gully by a juggling Steve Waugh. It was a dismissal that created a great deal of controversy. After the match I was told that television replays indicated the ball *may* have hit the ground before Steve completed the catch. I couldn't accept that. From my position at first slip I had an excellent view of the catch — and at no time did it seem to me that the ball had hit the ground. I believe that Steve and I both play the game fairly and if either of us had had any doubt that the catch was not a fair one we would have recalled Brian to the crease. Out in the middle there was no controversy. Steve, Brian and I all thought that Tug had fairly caught the ball, and Brian walked off. End of story.

We ended up knocking them over for 195 which was a terrific effort. All the guys chipped in. Brendon Julian got four wickets and bowled particularly well, and I was very happy with Glenn McGrath who really put it to their tail. We had talked about being aggressive with all their batsmen, including the tail, and Glenn was just that. Their tail didn't last long at all.

Then we went in, and at stumps had moved along to 2-91. I'm still there on 42, after a day I guess that I won't soon forget. I took four catches in their innings to make it the sort of day an opening batsman-captain crosses his fingers and hopes will happen at the start of every series. I couldn't really have asked for too much more. I didn't bat all that well, but I hung in there and to be 42 not out overnight was a good beginning. Slats got 18 before he was out to a very good catch at backward point, and Boonie went for 20, hooking at Courtney Walsh. We made fairly slow progress, due mainly to the fact that I was struggling, a bit below best form. When you're a touch off form you tend to concentrate harder, really put your head down. That was the way of things with me today.

So a good day for all of us. But I'm not about to get cocky. In Barbados in the corresponding Test last tour we bowled them out for 149 and were 2-56 at stumps. We ended up collapsing for 134, they went on to make 536 and we got a pretty fair hammering.

Around the Rockley Resort tonight there's a lot of talk about what a good day we had, how we're going to knock them off in three days, etc, etc. I don't want to hear about it. I'll be stressing to the guys in the morning that we've really got to knuckle down now — that tomorrow is a very, very important day. We are playing on a wicket that is going to break up. There's not a lot of grass on it, and with the prospect of batting last we're going to need a good lead.

Against the West Indies we always try to head for a total of 300-plus. This time 350-400 would be really great . . . without being greedy. For that to happen, someone has to make a big score. Hopefully it will be me, but if not me, someone has to do it. A big hundred. If we can do that and get a good lead and put their batting under pressure I believe we can win. The one thing I do know is that there's a long way to go.

APRIL 1

Overall, day two of the Test was a good one for us. It could have been better, could have been worse. Starting at 2-91, we ended up all out for 346. I got out just when I was starting to hit the ball well, at 55. That was pretty much the story of the day. Mark Waugh made a good 40, brother Steve an equally good 65, Brendon Julian a handy 31 and Ian Healy a brilliant 74 not out to strengthen things at the end. Everyone got *some* but no-one made the really big score that we have been talking about. At least we've got a useful lead of 151.

At stumps they were 0-13 off fifteen overs. We couldn't get the breakthrough we needed. But so far this game has gone pretty well. I suppose if someone had said to me before the game that after the first innings we would have been 150 runs up I would have said thank you very much.

They bowled very steadily today, with a good line and length. At times we lost wickets when we shouldn't have. But that's Test cricket. My innermost thoughts now are that we can win the game. We need to bowl well tomorrow — to take

SHAUN BOTTERILL/ALLSPORT•AUSTRALIAN PICTURE LIBRARY

Fast bowler McGrath and Curtly Ambrose exchange pleasantries at Barbados.

wickets and at the same time keep the runs down. If we chase anything under 200 in the second innings, I think we'll get them. Their bowling is nowhere near as penetrating as it used to be.

APRIL 2

It's late at night, and I'm just back in my room. In fact the day has clicked over, and we're into 3 April. I won't disclose the exact time. Let's just call it 'late'. Tonight we celebrated aboard the harbour cruiser *Bajun Queen*, really kicked our heels up after bringing off an incredible victory. It was my sixty-third Test match, and undoubtedly the best I have ever played in.

Today was a great day for Australian cricket, and a great day for everyone fortunate enough to have been involved in it. We knocked them over for a hundred and . . . I don't know . . . a hundred and ninety, or something. We needed 39 to win, and Slats and I knocked them off. None down. We've beaten the Windies by ten wickets.

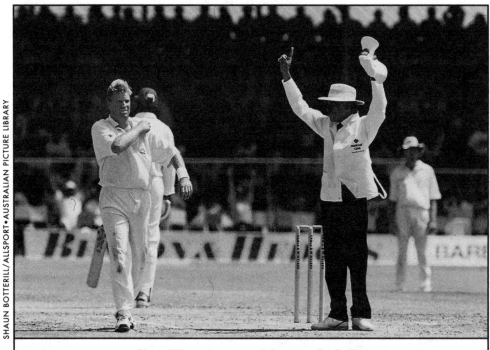

Shane Warne gets swatted for six at Barbados.

The guys just bowled superbly. Glenn McGrath was man of the match and deservedly so. I remember before the game that I mentioned several times how adversity often brings out the best in individuals (and teams). Well, the fact that injury knocked Damien Fleming and Craig McDermott out of the tour has led to the rest of the guys giving it all they've got and becoming even better bowlers than they were before. Glenn McGrath, Brendon Julian and Paul Reiffel . . . all three of them were outstanding in this match. Glenn was super today. He took five wickets and bowled as quick as anyone in the match. Brendon got four in the first innings, and Paul 1-15 today in eleven tight overs.

Warnie got three, and five wickets for the game. But for the first time in a while he wasn't 'the star' — and that's a great sign for the team that the workload is being shared. It was our *other* bowlers who were the stars. Today we just played great. We held our catches and the one that Steve Waugh took to get rid of Junior Murray was nothing short of fantastic.

The feeling is . . . well, pretty close to disbelief. We've knocked the West Indies over within three days, and I really can't find the words to express how I feel. It's the best Test match I've played in, and I've been in a few good ones, including the one at Manchester in 1989 when we regained the Ashes. Today beats that. I'll never forget it.

I'm enormously proud of the guys and I know now that we have what it takes to go on and win the series. But the game changes again now. We went into this Test as 9-2 outsiders. Now we've won it, and the pressure is on us. Suddenly people are saying: 'Hey, these Australians aren't too bad.' If we snuck up on them for this Test, through, we won't be able to do it next time. But if we can just keep doing what we've done these past three days, we can beat these blokes. They have some outstanding individuals, no doubt about that, but we are the better team.

APRIL 3

I'm not game to go back through last night's tape. I hope it made sense. It was (very) late and I was . . . well, let's face it . . . drunk! And why not after such a day? Today has been a recovery day. It's four o'clock in the afternoon and I'm down at the beach, doing some swimming and sobering up. I'm still pinching myself. This is the rest day in the Test, or would have been — and the game's already over! And we've won! Today I've been going back over it in my mind. I certainly had the feeling that things had come right before the Test, that spirit, form and intensity were lifting nicely to the required levels.

From what I have already said, I think it'll be clear that I can't give the bowlers a big enough wrap. There wasn't a lot of experience there, apart from Warnie, — and yet we were able to bowl them out twice in three days. It took us only forty-eight overs in the first innings and seventy-one in the second against the team which is supposedly the best in the cricketing world. I felt that at different stages our pacemen were all as quick as theirs. Paul Reiffel is probably the slowest of our three seamers, but he was hitting the bat hard and getting some bounce. The guys just seemed to have it in them this game. If we can maintain that we're going to be hard to beat.

The thing we've got to be ready for now is them coming back, because that's what they're going to try to do, for sure. They'll be hurting right now, and they are a team who have shown plenty of times the ability to fight back, and fight back hard. We've got to keep it going and keep the pressure on them. If things aren't going well for them, the local press will start calling for heads to roll and that can only be good for us.

It's funny when I think back. The only thing we lost in this match was the toss. And it was a toss that I *desperately* wanted to win. I thought winning the toss would give us the chance to use what I thought was going to be our strength in this match — our batting. My personal plan was for us to get plenty of runs on the board and then for the bowlers to bowl good line and length, applying pressure because of the runs we had on the board. We'd back that up with good fielding. That was the game plan, but you can tear it up. It was the bowlers who set up this game for us. We batted well, without batting *extra* well. To have to get 200 on the last day wouldn't have been easy. The West Indians have a reputation for winning games that look beyond winning. When England were here last time the Windies bowled them out for 46 when they were chasing only 194 to win the match. Our bowling was so good this time they were lucky to even make us bat again. The bowling was great, the catching fantastic.

Faxes have been rolling in all day, and that's always nice — to realise that something you have achieved far away has created good feelings and appreciation back home. Shane Warne's mum and dad Keith and Bridget always send me a fax before and after a Test match, and I appreciate that. Right through the tour so far Australians have materialised from everywhere. There are plenty of Aussies over here, and last night was a big back-slapping night. We really appreciate the support. It's great to have it at any time, but especially when you have a win.

Because of the quick fix in this Test we've got a few days to relax, and the chances are there'll be some more back slapping again. The next training session is booked for Wednesday, in two days' time, when we start preparations for the second Test in Antigua beginning on Saturday.

As has been well reported back home, the only bad news concerns our coach, Bob Simpson, who's been in hospital for a couple of days with a blood clot in his leg. He's in reasonable spirits, and was really bucked by the Test result — but his illness is a worry to us all. The word is that he's got to stay there for a week or so, so they can stabilise his condition. If he's okay then he'll resume travelling with us, but only in a managerial role. I doubt if he'll be doing too much coaching — let alone hitting high balls for us at fielding practice and yelling at us to get under them. It's now mid-afternoon, and I have a feeling the night could be a tricky one . . .

You wouldn't want to know it. I spent yesterday sobering up after the Test . . . and last night it happened all over again. Before the evening unfolded I called in to see Bob Simpson and found him in good spirits. The day after the Test our bus drove past the Queen Elizabeth Hospital where he is recuperating and we were all hanging out the windows yelling 'Simmo, we've beaten them! One-nil, one-nil' etc, etc . . . the way fifteen slightly inebriated guys might do. He told me last night that he'd heard a bit of a commotion . . .

Later I went for a feed with Boonie, Slats and Mark Waugh, after which they wisely departed and went home to catch up on some sleep. I had arranged to meet some friends of mine from school — Scott Bennett, who was in my form at Chatswood High School, Scott Corkran, who was a year ahead of me, and a few of their mates who are over here on a supporters' tour. I went to meet them for one beer at the Ship Inn.

Well, that one beer turned into a 3.30 a.m. epic. This time when I got home I made the shrewd decision not to turn on the tape. I reckoned two nights in a row was a bit much.

Aussie fans provided great support to the team in the first Test triumph at Barbados.

APRIL 4

Today, history has repeated itself — a sobering-up exercise, interrupted by the arrival of last night's revellers for an Australia v Trinidad golf contest around the Rockley Resort course. I was elected match referee, and walked around with them and had a couple of beers. I'm supposed to be meeting them again tonight at the Ship Inn. But enough is enough. It's time for me to get some proper sleep and to start focusing on the days ahead. It's Tuesday night. The serious business starts again tomorrow when we train at Kensington Oval. Then on Thursday we take off to Antigua, followed by a final training session on Friday before the Test next day.

Tomorrow I plan a team meeting, just a quick chat to get everyone fully back on course. We've had two days off, and I've valued and enjoyed the break as much as anyone. I think we earned it, too. But it's over now.

APRIL 5

Training today was good, although fairly relaxed. In the afternoon I went deep-sea fishing with Boonie, Greg Blewett and Ricky Ponting, aboard a boat provided for us by the Barbados Tourist Commission. We caught nothing but a barracuda and a kind of tuna known as skipjack. I was originally scheduled to go out with Scott Bennett and his team, but I felt obliged to go along with the

Tourist Commission invitation. Scott rang me tonight and told me he had caught four nice-sized dolphin fish. It was about the only disappointment of the Barbados leg of the journey, and a small one at that, so I can't complain. I think everyone will be a bit sad to leave Barbados. It's been good for us. We started the tour here, and it's been a sort of home base for us in between hopping from island to island. We lost the first one-day game here, admittedly, but it was a photo-finish match — and it was right then that we started to think the West Indies were beatable. They didn't quite seem to have the firepower of old. We gained a lot of heart from that match a month ago and this week it all came together for us in the Test win.

I called to see Simmo tonight at the hospital. He's making progress and will join us in Antigua on Monday. While there I also dropped off a T-shirt which had been signed by all the players to an Australian bloke who was knocked down by a taxi on Sunday night after the win. He broke an arm and both legs and will be in hospital for two weeks before flying back to Australia escorted by a nurse. His tour is finished. Obviously he's not in the best of spirits and when I heard about his misfortune I got the guys to autograph a shirt for him. I hope it gives him a lift.

So I've got mixed feelings tonight. Last night in Barbados. We won a great Test match for Australia here, and I guess all of us will always remember that.

APRIL 6

We ran into some almost routine hitches as we headed from Barbados to Antigua today. First, an early start (wake-up call 5.45 a.m.), only for the flight to be delayed. Meanwhile there had been a good deal of trouble over our hotel arrangements. We found out last night that instead of being booked into Halsion Cove we've been switched to the Royal Antiguan Hotel where we stayed in 1991. For some reason there have been some last-minute changes — which are all a bit strange, but don't matter too much. The Royal Antiguan is a good spot, although the service can be a bit rickety.

This afternoon Errol Alcott and I organised something completely different — a mini-triathlon down on the beach. We had two-man teams and a contest which included a run, a swim and a kayak paddle. Guess who won? Yep, Messrs Healy & Taylor and it was bloody hard work, especially the last swim after the kayaking. It was fun, but it was a bit more important than that. My idea has always been to keep the team 'together', and to get plenty of enjoyment out of the experience of this tour. Today was about that.

Our team meeting lasted only twenty minutes, but it was strong and positive. We're not complacent, but we know they're beatable. Tonight a new Australian record at our team dinner. Steve Waugh organised the night at a restaurant called the French Quarter and the bill came to US $1000 for a party of eighteen. An expensive night but a good one, with a lot of cricket talk buzzing around the table.

APRIL 7

Second Test eve. I think we're ready for what begins tomorrow at the St John's Recreational Ground, Antigua. Our final training today was at pretty ordinary facilities at the Police Ground — just a centre wicket on a pretty ordinary oval, the sort of place you'd play fourth or fifth grade in Sydney. But we made the most of it in front of a good crowd, the numbers on hand showing the interest that exists in tomorrow's Test. Fielding practice was good today. From training we went to the Recreational Ground itself, to set up our gear and have a quick fielding session there to get the 'feel' of the place.

This afternoon was spent relaxing, and waiting. I did some windsurfing, then lay around watching the second round of the US Masters on TV. I'm a lot more relaxed, less nervous than I was before the first Test. The way the guys played in Barbados has given me a lot of confidence in our ability. I feel I can't do any more as captain at this stage. I'm just looking forward to getting out there. We are a team with belief in ourselves at the moment. But I know only too well that the West Indians are very good at knocking the belief out of their opposition. Probably more than any other side they can bring you back a peg or two, and quickly. But we are ready, I think, and I hope we are going to play well over these next five days.

Tim May and Brendon Julian in the nets prior to the second Test at Antigua.

SHAUN BOTTERILL/ALLSPORT•AUSTRALIAN PICTURE LIBRARY

Chapter 5

SECOND TEST, ANTIGUA

APRIL 8

The first day of the second Test is over, and it went to them. It started badly when I lost the toss, although I sensed some uncertainty in Richie's reaction, as if he hadn't really decided what they were going to do. He obviously had some doubts. He ended up sending us in to bat. With two balls to go to the lunch break things were looking good. We were 0-82 and I was facing Curtly Ambrose. Then, in a moment I now regret, I went for a hook shot, and was caught down at fine leg. It was a nasty psychological blow on what turned out to be the last ball before the break. On the third ball after lunch, Slats fell, followed soon afterwards by Mark Waugh. Suddenly we were 3-89 and struggling. What had started to look like a great start was turning sour. Boonie and Tug (Steve Waugh) got through the next hour or so, but then they went in quick succession. Then after a series of leg-side catches, with Heals getting caught as I had, down at fine leg, we were all out for 216. At stumps they were 0-14.

One incident summed up the sort of day it was for us. With Paul Reiffel bowling to Stuart Williams, their opening batsman, I shifted Greg Blewett from cover to a catching position at bat-pad on the off side. The very next ball hit Williams' pad, deflected onto the bat, went straight to Greg . . . and he dropped it. It wasn't the easiest of chances, but it should have been taken. It would have been a great kick to us close to stumps, but it went to ground and so they're none down when they resume in the morning.

Not all is lost by any means. They worked hard and bowled bloody well today, far better than they did in Barbados. They really made us work hard for our runs. But, looking back, it was a day when a huge chance went begging. We had a chance to nail them, at 0-82, and unfortunately I was the one who started the rot, just before lunch. We've only got 216 on the board, but we've been bowling well and if we can keep the brakes on them and hold them to a reasonable score, then we might be able to give them something tough to chase on the last day.

Already the wicket is starting to play a bit low. I think their decision to send us in today was partly because they wanted to have a crack at us, but mostly because they were a bit worried about their batting. We need early wickets tomorrow to put them under pressure. If we can get those there's no reason why we can't bowl them out in the day. I'd like to see them chasing 200-plus on the fifth day, or even the fourth because I think on this wicket that could be very tough to get. The spirit in the side tonight was good, even though we didn't have a great day. Tomorrow we need good pressure bowling, good catching . . . and a dash of luck would be handy too. Mix up that lot and we're still in with a strong chance.

APRIL 9

We came back, just as I had hoped. In our talk before today's play I said to the guys: if we are a good side, this is the sort of day on which we have to show it. And we did. We bowled them out for 260, with Warnie and Paul Reiffel taking three apiece and Steve Waugh getting two very big wickets. Glenn McGrath got one and Brendon Julian one, so that everyone chipped in. The catching was excellent. I took three myself and Boonie grabbed a screamer to get rid of Brian Lara on 88. It was just the effort we needed to get us back in the ball game.

At stumps on day two we were 0-16. I'm on 4 and I've been hit from pillar to post. The Windies came out and bowled just the way I thought they'd bowl. They bowled short and quick — with two back for the hook, a bat-pad, three slips and a gully. If it wasn't intimidatory bowling, then I'm a bad judge. I faced around forty-five balls and I would suggest that somewhere between twenty and thirty of them were short-pitched. If they weren't bouncers, they sure were attempted bouncers.

It wasn't cricket. Honestly, I don't think the people over here know what cricket is half the time. All they want to see is short balls and blokes either hooking or ducking — or getting hit. That's what they seem to think cricket is about. And it's a damned shame because there's a hell of a lot more to cricket than that.

Anyhow, the good news is that Slats and I are both still there. We were 44 behind on the first innings, and we've got rid of 16 of those, so it's not far off being a line ball. My feeling tonight is that if we can bat well tomorrow and set them some sort of target, then we can win the cricket match. Having been out there, I wouldn't fancy batting last on this pitch. It's getting lower, and slower.

My feeling is that they've got problems in their side, and our job is to make those problems come to light in the next three days. But there's a long way to go — and the certainty of tomorrow is that they'll come out and throw everything at us.

What happened this afternoon when we went back in to bat is characteristic of cricket over here. I remember in the first Test of 1991, the two sides were getting on okay. Then the second came along and they were right into us with the short stuff. It gets you going — it really does. Today I was feeling quite punchy when I walked off the field.

I'm not a coward by any means. I never back away from the short stuff and the bruises tonight let me know that I've taken a few today. But to me the fundamental thing is that intimidatory tactics are not what the game of cricket is all about. This is beyond cricket. My great hope now is that we can win here and prove a point that there's more to cricket than just short-pitched bowling and intimidatory tactics. There are ways of getting guys out without trying to scare them out first.

The sort of bowling we saw today puts pressure on the umpires. The rules of cricket now dictate that a maximum of two bouncers per over are allowed. It's up to the umpires to decide what is a bouncer and what's not. Technically a bouncer is a ball that passes over shoulder height. But on this sort of wicket where the ball is tending to skid on, not all attempted bouncers are getting up. Therefore a guy can bowl three, four, five or even six attempted bouncers per over and get away with it — because only two might rise above the 'regulation' shoulder height.

To me it's a classic case of when the old rule relating to intimidatory bowling should be enforced. I think there's a real fine line in the whole thing — and if cricket administrators don't look at it seriously then the game is going to be ruined. The Antiguan crowd today were cheering and waving and carrying on when the barrage was underway. All these people know about is fast bowling, they don't know about *cricket.*

Against these tactics the batsman has two choices — to duck and weave, or to hook. But to hook the ball when there are two blokes back is a dangerous option. So there's more ducking and weaving than anything else going on, and the crowd thinks it's great. I don't. I don't think it's what cricket is about. I think it's cricket at its very lowest level. Bouncers are part of the game — and part of a bowler's arsenal. It's been that way in the past and will be in the future. But they shouldn't be a bowler's only weapon and be allowed to dominate the game.

APRIL 10

Day three of what is a very intense Test match was a good one for us — if personally disappointing for me. I was out early, for 5 . . . trying to hook again. It's the way it goes. That's twice I've been out that way, but I'm not going to stop. I've set out to attack these blokes and that's exactly what I'm going to keep doing. We lost Slats just before we knocked off the deficit of 44 and things weren't looking that great. But David Boon and Mark Waugh then came together and batted superbly, putting on 90. We are now 2-134, with a lead of 90 to take into the fourth day.

The West Indies bowlers again bowled short and sharp early on, but once the zip went out of their bowling they could no longer intimidate us, and Mark and David both looked pretty comfortable in the afternoon session. Both Slats and I went to short balls — he was caught at third slip, defending, *and* as I said, I was out hooking. I think that today's play left no doubt that we have more variety in our bowling attack. They appeared short on ideas, apart from an approach based on physical intimidation. The Windies' tactics in this match have been the subject of much discussion these past couple of days. Interestingly we have had comments from a few local people that they don't see what is going on as having very much to do with cricket either. They see it just as the West Indies fighting back (at 1-nil down), but fighting back with brutality rather than great cricket.

APRIL 11

Today was a rest day, and a quiet one. We had a function last night at a place called Fingers with the people from Cable and Wireless. I phoned my wife, and then a radio station back home — I think it was 3UZ in Melbourne — did an interview during which they hooked me up for a talk with a woman on board one of the boats in the America's Cup Challenge, which I was watching on TV at the same time! The wonders of modern science. I was talking to her about the America's Cup and she was talking to me about cricket. Apart from that it was a day of getting ready, mentally, for what lies ahead.

APRIL 12

A real hard-fought day of Test cricket today, missing segments here and there due to rain. It's a tough Test — we're 7-273 overall, with a lead of 229 and a day to play. The rain probably helped us more than it helped them. By reducing the time available, it means that their chances of winning the game are slowly fading. Time is running out. Tomorrow hopefully we can make another 40 or 50, then have a real good go at them. If we have them there for 70 overs, chasing 280, that will be great — because that way only we can win. We're in good shape. The rain is hanging about and maybe it will have the last say in this Test.

This was one of those days on which we had chances to get right on top, but couldn't quite drive it home. Once again, no-one made the really big score. Mark Waugh and David Boon both got 60s, then Greg Blewett got bogged down against Carl Hooper and was out in the over before lunch for 19. Heals and Tugger carried it on well, putting on about 60 before a rain break. Two overs after the resumption Healy was out, caught in slips. It was a frustrating sort of day. Each time we looked like grabbing the game by the throat and working it into a position in which we couldn't lose, we lost a wicket. But I'm certainly not disappointed. We're 229 up, Steve Waugh is still there on 52, and there are more runs to come. I have my fingers crossed for a full day's play tomorrow. The wicket is starting to take a bit of turn, and that's a good sign for us.

APRIL 13

Today was one of those days after which you think back on what might have been. It rained very heavily last night and when we got down to the ground it wasn't under water — but it was bloody wet. The final day of the Test didn't get going until 1.30 p.m., leaving time, as it turned out, for just forty-seven overs. I did what a captain has to do, and made a decision — that we'd keep going for a while, and bat them out of the game. I declared at ten past two, leaving them thirty-six overs to make 250-odd. They were never going to get the runs . . . and we were never going to bowl them out. So what could have been a really great Test match petered out into a dull old draw. The good news of course is that we remain one-nil up. We have played the Windies on two of their favourite grounds, Barbados and Antigua, and we lead one-nil. Not bad.

APRIL 14

Another travel day — a short flight this time, from Antigua to St Kitts. On arrival we had time for a splash in the hotel pool before heading to the golf course. A game of golf is something I look forward to a great deal on tour. Today quite a few of us played, including Boonie, Justin Langer, Greg Blewett, Ricky Ponting, Mark Waugh and Glenn McGrath. The competition is never less than fierce. Ricky and Greg both play off 5 and 4 handicaps respectively, so it's tough going against them. Today a couple of Brisbane ex-pats also joined us for the round. Tomorrow, the last practice match before Tests 3 and 4 — against a Board XI.

APRIL 15

As per bloody usual I lost the toss to start the match against the Board XI at Basseterre, St Kitts. So we had to bowl on a real belter of a wicket, but at the end of the day we'd come out of it pretty well. Rain cut into the day to some extent, but by stumps we had them 8-209. Carl Rackemann got three for 40-odd and Tim May two for 40-odd and they were the only two blokes I wanted to see bowl. Both bowled steadily, and the wickets will lift their spirits. We enjoyed the day, although there were some catches put down. I dropped one, Mark Waugh dropped one and Tim May dropped one. It's funny to be out there really. All we're thinking about is the third Test, and that's some distraction. But the guys are still reasonably motivated, although it's a different spirit out there on the field — more relaxed, with some jokes flying around. We're not fully wound up, but we're still playing good cricket, and I'm pleased about that. We're keen to win, too. We'd love to knock these last two over early and have a dig on what is a really good batting wicket. We're still thinking we can win the game, even though I managed to lose a toss it would have been good to call right.

Tonight a cocktail party around the swimming pool at the hotel. Not a bad life, this cricket touring. We talked about cricket and a lot of other things, and just relaxed.

Mark Taylor and Bob Simpson on Simpson's return from hospital —
during the Antigua Test.

APRIL 16

They came out swinging this morning. A guy named Otis Gibson who batted ten for the Board XI but should be batting a hell of a lot higher made 50-odd in quick time and smashed us around the park for a while. They finished up with 261, and at stumps we were 5-278. Greg Blewett made 93, I got 62, Slats made 60 and Babsie is 24 not out. It was a pretty fair day for us. They were doing quite a bit with the ball and I struggled a bit, just didn't hit it too well, but I was out there for a while, and it was a good solid session. Poor old Justin Langer got nought in his first game for about four weeks, so it was a shame for him. It can be a cruel game at times.

At the end of the day's play our bus didn't turn up, and there was a bloke hanging around the dressing sheds who was drunk, probably stoned too, and sporting a cane-knife. We were pretty wary of him — but at least there were some security guys around.

I had a bit of a run-in with a guy from the local St Kitts Association about the fact that our bus wasn't there. The bus for the opposition turned up about five minutes after the end of the day's play. Forty minutes later the same bus came back and picked us up. It was a pretty rough deal, and I let him know I wasn't too happy about it. As I mentioned before, if the same thing happened to a West Indies team in Australia, there would be hell to pay. It was no big deal, but niggling. But by tonight we were all pretty relaxed when a group of us had a meal down at a place called The Anchorage. Tomorrow morning we've got *official* team photos to be taken at the ground and on the way there we're going to organise some *unofficial* team shots. It should be good fun.

APRIL 17

The final day of the game was a real fizzer. I decided to bat on rather than talk to their captain about us maybe declaring, and them setting us some sort of target to chase late in the day. It might have been the better option. As it was we only lasted about an hour. Boonie was out in the second over of the morning. Mark Waugh hung around to make 30 not out and everyone else fell by the wayside. All out 317. Then they batted for the rest of the day, finishing with six for 253 after being one for 194 at one stage late in proceedings. It was pretty much a non-event, a real 'nothing' game, although we got some handy batting practice along the way.

By tonight the game was forgotten. All the talk in the bar was of the Test match, which is now just three days away, in Trinidad. Tomorrow it gets deadly serious when we have our team meeting, and then a team dinner, the two things together designed to have everyone switched right back on. I won't have too much to say. It was obvious tonight that the guys are focused and really looking forward to the game. There is now a strong belief in this team that we are going to beat them in this series. Knowing the Windies, I'm sure they still believe they can beat us, too . . .

There have been a lot of comparisons made between the situation now and the series in Australia in 1992-93 when the West Indians came from one-nil down to win 2-1. But this time it's different. On that earlier tour there was a feeling that the West Indies were getting on top coming into the fourth Test. This time, that's not the case. These last two Tests will be fiercely fought, but we've got our noses in front and there is no sign this time that they are in the ascendancy as they were in 1992-93.

The photo sessions this morning were voted something of a success. We had one team shot taken in the pool bar out the front of the hotel, and a couple on top of the mountain which looks down over Basseterre. They should be good mementos of what seems to be building into a pretty special tour.

APRIL 18

Today was just another regulation nightmare travel day: We left the hotel in Basseterre at 9.45 a.m. for an 11.15 charter flight to Trinidad; the plane was an hour late; at 4 p.m. we were still at Trinidad Airport. Bags which we had sent direct from Antigua after the second Test hadn't been cleared by Customs in the ensuing four days. So we had to troop across to another section of the airport to get someone to clear the bags for us; then we couldn't get the coffins on the bus. They had to follow us later; as I said, just another regulation nightmare travel day. Tonight, a beer, a club sandwich and a Tom Cruise movie on the in-house channel at the Trinidad Hilton.

APRIL 19

It's late in the evening, with thirty-six hours or so to go to the Test. We had a solid build-up today to the next great challenge of the tour, although the rain that has been hanging around Trinidad meant that the practice wickets we used for this afternoon's session were below par. They were damp, and under-prepared. But I hit the ball pretty well, and I'm confident about my own form heading towards the Test.

Everything else was fine. I opened the team meeting up to the other guys, rather than hogging it myself — and there were some good thoughts, reflecting a strong and positive attitude within the team. The team dinner reinforced the good vibes from this afternoon's meeting. We sat down for dinner at 7.30 p.m. and we were still there at eleven . . . talking cricket. I think we're ready or close to it. If the West Indies are going to beat us this time they're going to have to be on their very best behaviour. Stopping off for one quick beer before bed I ran into AB (Allan Border) and Deano (Dean Jones) in the bar. They're over here working with Prime Sports Network and it was good to see them. I stayed a little bit longer than I had intended and the one beer turned into several.

They'd been to the Masters in the US and filled us in on that. Not surprisingly, AB seemed keen to talk about the Shield final after, Queensland's first-ever victory. Their good wishes are with us all the way in this one. It's been a really good day. The only unsettling thing as we head into this match is the weather. There's been a fair bit of rain, and the predictions are that it will be hanging around for the next two weeks. I hope the forecasters are wrong. Given the full quota of match hours I think we can beat the West Indies here and go ahead two-nil. Time, of course, will have the final word on that opinion.

APRIL 20

It's the night before the Test, and I believe our preparation has been better than theirs. We had a good training session today even though the nets here have been terrible. They are wet, under-prepared and very ordinary wickets — below the standard required for getting ready for Test match cricket. We have done our best to make the most of what we have been offered. I have a very clear memory of the West Indies in 1991-92 complaining very strongly about the patchy state of the Sydney wickets. Yet there is absolutely no doubt that on tour in Australia they get a much better deal than we do here — in wickets, travel and accommodation.

We practised this morning — had a hit and a bowl, then concentrated on some fielding. Their session was scheduled for this afternoon, but the rain came and they had to cancel their plans. So we've had a better lead-in, which is a nice little 'edge'. The spirit at training today was excellent, notwithstanding the state of the wickets. Everyone put in really hard. Without doubt we are a bigger threat to them this time than on the last tour . . . and they know it.

I have just knocked back an interview request from a bloke in New Zealand. It's 9.30 on the night before the Test, too late for that. I have fulfilled my media commitments the very best I can right through. But on Test-match eve you have to draw the line somewhere. Tonight I watched the America's Cup Challenger Series and saw the Aussie boat go down to the New Zealanders. I hope it wasn't an omen.

The major problem for this Test remains the weather. It's very hot and sticky and threatening and I don't know whether it's going to allow us five days' play. My own feelings tonight are a mixture of excitement and apprehension. I know that if I win the toss tomorrow then I'm going to have a very tough decision to make. With the overcast conditions and a damp wicket at Queen's Park Oval the temptation is there to send them in, something I don't usually like doing. Either way I've got a good feeling. If I do send them in I know we've got the bowlers to bowl them out. My main problem is winning the toss — which I don't usually do. I console myself with the thought that Richie Richardson is going through exactly the same process that I am. He'll be a bit uncertain about the wicket and the weather and what to do. The question is: whether you try to win it on the first day by knocking the other side over cheaply and then getting ahead, or whether you play the percentages and aim for victory on the final day. But I am feeling quietly confident.

Chapter 6

THIRD TEST, TRINIDAD

APRIL 21

The first day of the third Test match is over, and it wasn't a great one for Australia. It rained overnight and the wicket was . . . well, the best way to describe it is 'under-prepared'. It's soft, grassy and holding a lot of moisture. And as per usual I lost the bloody toss. That's six in a row now. They sent us in. Well, Slats got out in the second over and I got out in the third. When Mark Waugh went early too, we were 3-14. The day was plagued by rain and only thirty-nine overs were bowled. At the end of it we were 7-112 with Steve Waugh making a very gutsy 54 not out. He was dropped once and had his fair share of luck, but it was a terrific knock on a wicket like this one. Against a team bowling good line and length it's bloody hard to score on such a wicket, with the ball coming through very slowly.

One hundred and twelve runs. It doesn't look great, but there's a long way to go in this game. If the weather stays as it is, with the covers on a lot of the time, the wicket is going to retain its moisture and it will be tough for the batsmen the entire game. If the rain more or less stays away, there's certainly going to be a result and we are certainly still right in it. There are definite question marks over their batting; the highest score they have made so far is 260, and that on a good wicket.

The situation represents a big test for us. If we can come back and win from this first-day position against the West Indies then we are the best team in the world. No doubt about it. Our comeback level and our fighting ability in Antigua were outstanding. If we show the same qualities in this Test we're still in with a very good chance.

APRIL 22

Today, the comeback day we had hoped for. It's starting to become a bit of a habit. We ended up getting bowled out for 128, with Steve Waugh left on 63 not out after playing very well. There was still plenty in the wicket. It was still juicy. Before the morning's play started we had a chat, and reckoned that whatever we made, we'd have a good chance of bowling them out for around the same score. And that's how it turned out. We got them out for 136 and at stumps we were 0-20. So we're twelve runs in front with all ten wickets in hand. We've got our noses back in front — just. It really was a terrific day for us.

Glenn McGrath bowled superbly and finished with 6-47 — a memorable day for him. Paul Reiffel was just about as good. He took 2-26, but his figures could have been far better. Once again we held our catches. I took a couple myself, including one off Brian Lara which I was very happy to drag in. That was a big wicket for us.

This is developing into another outstanding Test. I know the West Indies will come out firing again tomorrow, as they always do, but if we can hold them off and bat well, get some sort of reasonable lead on the board — something over 200 would be good — then we're in with a great chance.

APRIL 23

Cricket can be an amazing game. Twenty-four hours ago I was here in the room, full of hope that we would go on and win the third Test. Tonight I am coming to terms with the fact that we have been beaten by nine wickets. We started twelve runs up, then Slats went in the second over, caught in the slips off one that was just about unplayable. Boonie and I soldiered on for a while and at one stage when I hit three fours in about eight balls I was starting to think that I had a chance of taking the game by the scruff of the neck. I hit Kenneth Benjamin for consecutive boundaries and then he got one to move away. I nicked it, and was gone for 30. Two for 52. Babsie went next over, and then the Waughs got together, put on 30, and at 3-85 we weren't looking too bad. Then, disaster. We went from 3-85 to 8-87 and ended up being all out for 105.

It wasn't much to chase. They played and missed a number of times early on, so the wicket was still doing a bit . . . although not nearly as much as our 105 would suggest. Then within the day it was over. They got the 98 they needed with the loss of only one wicket. I am still coming to terms with the fact that we were beaten so decisively — and it's really disappointing. I think a big opportunity has just passed us by.

The series of 1992-93 in Australia is in my mind. I think of Adelaide, where we led 1-0 in the series and had our opportunity to win the Test match. We lost by one run, and that squared the series with Perth only two days away. Well, this series is now all-square — and Jamaica is only four or five days away. We've got more time here than we had then — time to re-group, gather our forces, get ourselves back on track. The pendulum has swung their way, and the task for us is to swing it back again our way. The balance of power has changed constantly on this tour. They had it during the one-dayers, then we beat them by ten wickets in the first Test. The second Test went one way, then the other, and so did this one — until today when they had their best day of the series.

I'm disappointed in our batting. I really thought we had our minds switched on in that department. I was wrong. The batting here really fell down. What happened in the first innings was understandable. We batted on a wicket that was under-prepared and below standard. The fact that we bowled them out for 136 reaffirmed that. But today we were shooting for 250 or so, and we only made 105. We threw away an opportunity.

My confidence is no more than slightly bruised. I am convinced we are the better cricket team of the two. The wicket here suited them better than us — and that's cricket — but I hope we can get a flat, dry, hard wicket in Jamaica. In five days there we can still do what we came to do.

APRIL 26

I'm checking back in after a couple of days away from the recorder. I needed the time to freshen up, get my thoughts together. There's been some relaxing, some reflection, some talking — and the feeling, spirit and confidence in the side remain good. I've just been talking to one of the touring journos, Trent Bouts for *The Australian* about a piece he wants to do, on my thoughts on the intimidatory bowling law. I'm quite happy for him to do, it — because I genuinely don't believe the law is right at the moment or is doing the job that everyone wants it to do. I'm just a little concerned, though, with the timing of such an article. The feeling between the two sides in this series has been a hell of a lot better than it's been in the past and I don't want to ruin it by people thinking I'm whingeing about the West Indies bowling.

My major concern in this series, as I've already said, came when Slats and I had to face a real barrage in our second innings of the second Test in Antigua. Really, that was the only major problem. The cricket has been played in the right spirit. It's been good cricket. I really don't want to make a big scene of it before this last Test which is going to be a beauty. The timing is not ideal, but I have some strong thoughts on the subject and Bouts is keen to do a piece. So I did the interview.

We've had some good chances to relax these last couple of days. The people from Angostura, the rum makers, took us out on a boat trip to one of the islands off Trinidad. They barbecued a sheep, and we had some beer and rum. It was a good day, very relaxing. Then the same crowd took us for a golf day at the St Andrew's Club, which was good fun. That night a guy named Mark Chapman, who works for Angostura, invited Boonie, Slats and me up to his place in the hills, overlooking Port of Spain, and put on a barbecue. It was a very enjoyable

SHAUN BOTTERILL/ALLSPORT•AUSTRALIAN PICTURE LIBRARY

Curtly Ambrose leads the high-fives at the fall of another wicket during the Windies third Test triumph. Ambrose took 9 of his 13 wickets in the series at Queens Park.

evening. Not much else to report. Tonight, our last in Trinidad, we had a team trivia night which provided more than a few laughs. Then, early to bed. We're up at 4.30 in the morning for the trek to Jamaica, the last big hop before the Test match that will make us or break us.

APRIL 27

Today was a big travel day — the 6.45 a.m. flight from Trinidad, via Barbados, Antigua and St Martin's to Jamaica. It was 1.45 p.m. Jamaican time when we finally reached our hotel in Kingston. It was a long haul. By three o'clock we were on the training paddock at Sabina Park, a ground that has improved a hell of a lot over the last four years. The outfield is vastly better than what I remember. Morale in the side seems fairly good, although I'm a little worried about Warnie. He's got a bad thumb which is troubling him. I think it's something we've got to push him through. We really need him for this game. I've got a feeling that this is a wicket that will turn a bit, and if we are to have a chance of winning the Test match we need him there, and operating well. So I'll be working on him. I had a chat with him today to try to get his spirits up and I'll be doing the same tomorrow. I want to see him in this game with as much confidence as he can muster. Training was good — we didn't do too much, but it was sharp and enthusiastic.

I'm a little peeved with the press over here. The Jamaican press seem to have this thing about wanting to do individual interviews. Today they straggled up to me one by one, looking for interviews. I've got news for them. I can't be spending two or three hours a day doing interviews when we're getting ready for a Test. I spoke to our liaison people and suggested an overall press conference, and asked them to organise that for tomorrow. I'm not going to go through again what I went through today.

APRIL 28

In twelve hours we play a Test match that is crucial for both the Australian team, and for me as its captain. I've really enjoyed these last twelve months and I think the side has played pretty well under my captaincy. But a lot depends on what happens over these next five days. If we win this Test we go to No. 1 in the world, and everyone says I've done the job as captain. If we lose, well the status of the Australian team hasn't changed a hell of a lot. We've got everything to play for.

I've been a bit grumpy today. The morning started with a 6.30 a.m. phone call from a lady from the Jamaican Broadcasting Commission, which woke me and got me off on the wrong foot with the media. The press here have been the rudest group I have struck. They are constantly on the phone, and I've barely had a moment's peace since I've been here. At training today I was pretty grouchy, although I loosened up towards the end. I guess we're all just a bit on edge. Me too.

SHAUN BOTTERILL/ALLSPORT•AUSTRALIAN PICTURE LIBRARY

Courtney Walsh appeals unsuccessfully for the wicket of Mark Taylor,
third Test action at Queens Park.

CLIVE MASON/ALLSPORT•AUSTRALIAN PICTURE LIBRARY

Steve Waugh meets the press after his exchange with Curtly Ambrose in the third Test.

The guys are training well, but there's a slight hesitancy in the team. Just nerves I guess. We all realise that we have five days to make it happen, five days to make all the hard work worthwhile. It's been a good season, a good year and we all want to finish on a high note. We talked today about the fact of its being a five-day game. Two of the Tests so far finished in only three days, and the other was washed out. So everything has happened sort of quickly. I just reminded the guys that this one could be a long haul, and that there should be no panic.

Our big need is to make some runs, and to put some pressure on them batting last in the game. Winning the toss would be a *great* start. I'm sure they will clam up and look for the draw if they are under pressure towards the end. I did an interview with Jim Maxwell for ABC radio today, and caught up on some missing sleep this afternoon. It was a quiet night, a couple of early beers, then dinner. I'm feeling surprisingly relaxed, and looking forward to it. The statisticians tell me that I need only three more runs in this game to pass 5000 in Tests. I'm proud of that.

ABOVE *Brendon Julian, relaxing prior to battle early in the West Indies tour.* ALLSPORT•AUSTRALIAN PICTURE LIBRARY

ABOVE *Shane Warne captures the wicket of Phil Simmons in the first of the one-dayers at Kensington Oval.*

BEN RADFORD/ALLSPORT•AUSTRALIAN PICTURE LIBRARY

BELOW *Brian Lara cuts loose for 139 in the third limited overs international at Trinidad.*

BEN RADFORD/ALLSPORT•AUSTRALIAN PICTURE LIBRARY

Mark Taylor relaxing at St Vincent

ABOVE *Captain Mark Taylor celebrates an historic victory in the first Test at Kensington Oval.*

BELOW *Craig McDermott after injuring his ankle at Georgetown, Guyana.*

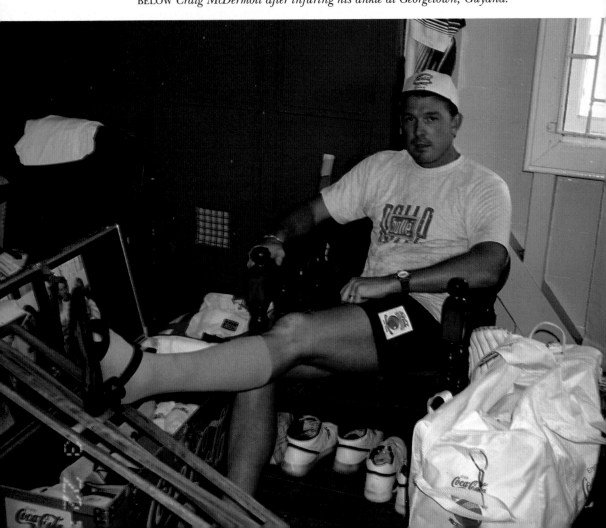

A very happy Ian Healy with his innovative Man of the Match award after the second One Day game at Port of Spain.

ABOVE *Taylor holds the ball aloft after the dismissal of Winston Benjamin off*
Shane Warne in the first innings of the Barbados Test. SHAUN BOTTERILL/ALLSPORT•AUSTRALIAN PICTURE LIBRARY
BELOW *Brendon Julian captures the wicket of Richie Richardson to give Australia just the start required.*
The Windies were 3 for 6 early in the first Test. SHAUN BOTTERILL/ALLSPORT•AUSTRALIAN PICTURE LIBRARY

Brian Lara during his innings of 88 at St John's, Antigua. The innings was his highest score of the series - by Lara's lofty standards a disappointing effort.

Mark Taylor holds his head after another near miss in Antigua. CLIVE MASON/ALLSPORT•AUSTRALIAN PICTURE LIBRARY

Glenn McGrath captures the wicket of Richardson to have the Windies reeling at 2 for 6 in their first innings at Queens Park. SHAUN BOTTERILL/ALLSPORT•AUSTRALIAN PICTURE LIBRARY

ABOVE *After the Trinidad Test the team went for a cruise around the islands. Seen here is skipper Taylor enjoying the prospect of some relaxation.*
BELOW *Michael Slater, Glenn McGrath and Mark Taylor soaking up the sun in Angostura.*

Captain Taylor, carried on the shoulders of jubilant team-mates at the conclusion of the fourth Test triumph.

CLIVE MASON/ALLSPORT•AUSTRALIAN PICTURE LIBRARY

The boys relax at the Frigate Bay Beach Resort, their hotel base at St Kitts.

King of all he surveys. Mark Taylor, the Frank Worrell Trophy and the people of Sydney.

Chapter 7

FOURTH TEST, JAMAICA

APRIL 29

I slept well, unusually for me before the first day of a Test, and awoke this morning to a fax from Prime Minister Paul Keating. The guys appreciated that. And then to battle . . .

The same old bloody story. I lost the toss. That means I've lost it in all four Tests, plus in the other three first-class games on tour. Seven consecutive tosses. Can you believe it? I've called seven tails, and it's come up heads seven times. I'm starting to wonder whether Richie is fiddling with that coin (just joking!!). Richie chose to bat, which was no major surprise.

We had a dream start — Paul Reiffel got Stuart Williams second ball, and we had them 1-0. But from then on until just before lunch they were pretty much in the ascendancy. Brian Lara was hitting the ball well, although with some luck via a couple of nicks that dropped short. But we got him just before lunch and they were 2-113 after a morning in which they had given our bowlers something of a pasting. We picked up two more wickets for about 80 in the session after lunch, then cleaned them up in the final session, taking 4-17 with the second new ball, and closing them down at 265. That was a darned good effort when you consider at one stage they were 1-103 and looking ominous.

The bowlers did a fine job for us collectively. Brendon Julian bowled better than he had been recently, and Warnie picked up 2-72 off twenty-five overs. It was a really good solid effort all round — and now it's up to us batsmen to build on that foundation. We need to bat bloody well tomorrow, and hopefully into the third day. I wouldn't like to be chasing too many runs against these blokes on the final day. They have a habit of knocking over teams batting last. Tomorrow is a huge, huge day. I reckon we need something up from 350 to 400 to be competitive. We need 100 per cent from everyone. We've talked about that — about steeling ourselves, about being gritty.

APRIL 30

It's 6.30 p.m. and what I've got to say I'm only going to say to this tape recorder. We've had a GREAT day, and gone a long way towards grabbing hold of the Frank Worrell Trophy. It didn't start out too well. I smashed a ball from Courtney Walsh straight at Jimmy Adams at bat pad and he held an absolute screamer of a catch. Taylor 8, Australia 1-17. It was a big personal disappointment, although at least I passed that 5000 runs milestone. Then Boonie went, caught behind off his helmet, and we were 2-50. I'll admit I was worried at that stage. I kept thinking back to the times we played these blokes and had opportunities and somehow they would *make* something happen — take a great catch or bowl an unplayable delivery to turn the game. Slats went at 73, hooking. He had never really looked like it. He seemed hell-bent on playing the hook, even with two blokes out in the deep, and they finally got him, caught on the boundary. We went to lunch at 3-91, with the Waughs both in. Before lunch I said to Mark, who was on 20, 'You're looking all right,' and he replied, 'Yeah, I feel pretty good. It might be time for me and Steve to put on another 464' — which they had done for New South Wales against Western Australia some four years before. I said to him, 'Mate, I'd be happy if you put on *two* — sixty-four'.

Well, Steve and Mark went out and put on 231. Mark finally went for 126, and at stumps Steve was still there on 110, with Greg Blewett on five or six. We're on 4-321, a lead of 56 with three days to go. We've got our heads in front again. Opportunity presented itself — and today we grabbed it. There was no celebrating. The guys had a beer or two each in the change rooms, then we came home to think about it. There's still a long way to go. We are playing a team which has great pride and great tradition. But . . . boy, it's looking promising. If we can squeeze another 100 or 150 and build the lead up to 200 or so we have a wonderful chance

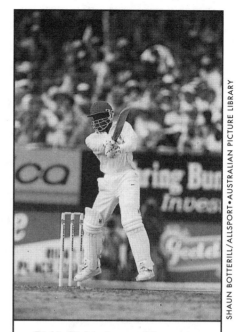

SHAUN BOTTERILL/ALLSPORT•AUSTRALIAN PICTURE LIBRARY

Richie Richardson on his way to a century in the fourth Test. It was, remarkably, the only 100 scored by a West Indian in the four-match series.

of taking the Test, and with it the series. We've got to give it everything we've got tomorrow. The next day is a rest day and ideally I'd love to see us poised at the end of the day's play tomorrow — ready to win it on day four or five.

MAY 1

It's actually a few minutes after midnight and I'm reflecting on a day that was nothing short of fantastic for us. We batted on to 531, with Steve Waugh getting a wonderful 200, and Greg Blewett contributing 69 in the morning session. Leading by 266 we then come out to take three huge wickets — Richardson, Lara and Stuart Williams. Paul Reiffel got the three of them — the prize wicket of Lara, LBW, with one that kept really low. They are 3-63, needing to make 266 to make us bat again. We are in a sensational position and all the guys are really pumped up, as you can imagine. I've spent the last half-hour back in the room going through all the faxes that have arrived from home. Obviously it's big news there and people are as excited as they are here. The day after tomorrow we have the chance to establish ourselves as the world's best cricket team. Tomorrow (or today, rather) we can relax, and wait. I'm sure we'd all prefer to be going straight back out there to try and finish it off.

We've got one hand on the trophy, as the saying goes. We've got to reach out yet with the other one, and that may be tougher than we think because these guys we're playing are proud people. They won't give it away easily.

Steve Waugh, Australia's player of the series, seen here driving during his magnificent innings of 200 in the fourth Test.

MAY 2

It rained all morning here, a great day for a rest day. We missed it because we had headed off early on a bus trip across to the other side of the island to have a look at the Dunne River Falls. We spent the day there, courtesy of the people from the Sandles hotel chain. I wasn't going to go, but I figured that if I didn't I'd only hang around here and run through all the *ifs* and *buts* in my head. It was better to be occupied elsewhere. We had some rain over there too, but it was a good day, and the trip and the lunch, etc, filled in the day nicely. We've been talking about winning the game. It's impossible not to. We just need the weather to be kind, for the rain to blow away and for May 3 to dawn fine and clear.

The support from back home has been terrific. I must have 250 faxes in my room now. Australia is cheering us on, and that feels good. My gut feeling is that we have broken the backs of our opposition. There are some fighters still to get past — Jimmy Adams, who is still there, will be a big wicket if and when we get him. Warnie and I had a beer tonight and a good chat. Greg Ritchie was in the bar and was a bit remorseful about the fact that he'd run out onto the ground when Steve got his 200. He'd had a couple of drinks at the time. He apologised to me but there was no need for that — I thought it was quite funny, just an overflowing of enthusiasm. I think the only problem Greg has got is coming to terms with himself.

I'm hoping to get a fair night's sleep, but I guess the chances of that aren't too strong. I've got my fingers crossed for a nice dry ground . . . a ground on which seven wickets will fall.

MAY 3

It's 9.20 p.m. and I'm finally back in my room. I still haven't showered since leaving the ground. A few hours ago we won the fourth Test match by an innings and 50 runs . . . or was it 52?. . . who cares!! The Frank Worrell Trophy is sitting in my room.

What a day it was. What a day! We made mistakes today that we haven't made all series. We dropped some catches, we did a few things wrong. But we got through — we won the match, the series and the Trophy. The talk is that we can stand tall as the best cricket team in the world. And to have been captain of that team through this crowded year has been a privilege and an honour — and something I will never forget for the rest of my life. I really feel that whatever I may achieve from now on in world cricket is a bonus, because I've achieved everything I wanted to achieve.

Today was just an outstanding day, despite the few fumbles. I took the last catch, to get rid of Kenneth Benjamin, and I hung onto the ball and gave it later to Bob Simpson. I reckon he deserves it for the amount of effort he has put into Australian cricket. I grabbed a stump as a souvenir, got my press commitments out of the way after the game, then just relaxed in the dressing room. We spent hours there after the match, somehow reluctant to leave — the whole team, together with blokes like Allan Border, Dean Jones, David Hookes and Geoff Lawson. They're all part of this. Today wasn't about one day, or one series or one year or one team. It was about *Australian cricket*. Perhaps the fifteen tourists of 1995 will be remembered as having done something sort of *legendary*, but

Ecstatic Aussie fans invade the pitch as Australia wraps it up.

today was also about all the days that have built up to this, and all the players who have been part of that.

I'm back in my room just sitting here looking at the trophy. The little silver badges on it tell me that 1975-76 was the last time we won it. We lost it in 1978, and haven't seen it since. I'm just sitting here, enjoying a quiet moment, and letting it all wash over me . . .

Paul Reiffel savours the moment as he takes the wicket of Winston Benjamin to wrap up victory for Australia.

MAY 4

It's the day after the Test, or late at night to be precise. I didn't get much sleep last night. I got to bed around 1.30 a.m., but I was up again soon after six. The adrenaline still pumping I guess. I felt okay, too — just a little bit hungover, which wasn't too surprising. The faxes have rolled in in vast numbers today — from Paul Keating, John Howard, and various State Premiers all the way down to some from schoolkids. And they are the most important ones, no doubt. One of our jobs as Australian cricketers is to present it as a game that kids will love, and want to play. To get a bundle of faxes from the kids back home is just great.

It's been a fantastic day. I went to the Constance Springs Golf Club with AB and Boonie and a few of the younger guys — Justin Langer, Glenn McGrath and Ricky Ponting — who played in a threesome behind us. I played my worst golf in a long time, but enjoyed every minute of it. We even ran into a big rainstorm and got drenched. Who cares?

Tonight the journos put on drinks around the pool for us and we appreciated that. But I'm just about gone, absolutely knackered. I've had a few beers, but it's a lot more than that. I guess it's all the emotion and the tension pushing through. It really has been a huge forty-eight hours.

Tonight I'm thinking that I've been away too long. I spoke to my wife on the phone and she said all the calls and all the reactions back home had been fantastic. Apparently they're talking about a motorcade to welcome us back, and that's exciting. It's all very special. Within the team, and within the hotel generally, the smiles are a mile wide, and permanently fixed. We're off to Bermuda, of course, and that will be fun. Probably we'll spend the two weeks telling each other how good we are. We might as well enjoy it while we can. Later this year, it all starts again . . .

MAY 6

It's 1 a.m. and I've lost some time somewhere along the way. Just home from a very good night out put on by the guys from the electronic media. They had us in a room downstairs, showing us the blooper tapes — of some of my interviews which I stuffed up, of things that *they* stuffed up. It was a good time. Very funny. Afterwards they shouted us out to a meal at a Chinese restaurant, followed by some (more) drinks at a nearby club.

In some ways tonight is bitter-sweet. It's the last time I'll be talking into the tape from the West Indies. We're off to Bermuda in the morning for the

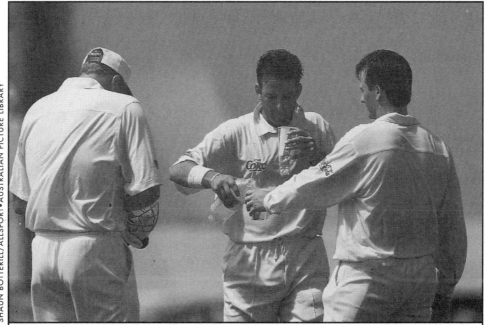

Mark and Steve Waugh pause for refreshments during their 231 stand in the final Test.

wind-down section of the tour. My day-to-day diary will finish on this tape — but I'll certainly be adding some reflections on Bermuda, and especially on the tour, and why it worked so well.

Golf was on the agenda this last day. Boonie and I took on Mark Waugh and Shane Warne at Constance Springs. With four holes to play we were three down. But we took the last four holes. What a finish! It was a pleasant way to kill four hours, and that's one of the reasons I like to play golf on tour. It's enjoyable, it fills in some time, and it takes you away from the grind of day-to-day hotel life.

There are a lot of emotions going on at the moment. Homesickness is one of them. I miss my family. I miss them a lot. I was watching a film on the TV today which had Danny De Vito looking after his two kids, and I must admit I got a bit teary. I'm not looking for any fuss when I get home. I'm mainly looking for some quiet time with the family. They are the people who are important to me. I love playing this game, really love it — but my family are, and always will be, my main priority in life. They are often pushed into the background, but that won't be the case when I get home. I'm going to have to do some juggling with the celebrations, the pats on the back, the time spent with sponsors and so on, and mix all that in what I really want to do, spend some time with the family.

Chapter 8

REFLECTIONS ON A MAGIC TOUR

A great many things crowd into my mind when I look back on the tour. This pretty relaxing time in Bermuda has given me a chance to reflect on the shortcomings and, ultimately, the achievements of these past weeks.

Overall it has been a triumph against some odds. We were a little flat in the one-dayers, but I believed all along that it was 'one-day staleness' and not an overall problem with the spirit of the physical fitness of the team. Then to lose both Damien Fleming and Craig McDermott was a real kick in the guts. A combination of those things probably had people back home ready to draw a line through our chances straightaway. But even at the lowish point of those one-day losses we all had at the back of our minds the thought that we were here for something different. We knew that people would remember the Test series, and that alone. The question was: could we lift enough to turn things around in the Tests?

The tour changed virtually on a single day. The practice session two days before the first Test in Barbados was as if someone had thrown a switch. It was unbelievable. All of a sudden the guys were buzzing. The quicks were running off the long run to bowl. Blokes were batting more sensibly. The fielding practice was of a much higher quality, much sharper, much quicker. The one-dayers were over and we were ready to knuckle down and play some serious cricket.

Maybe the West Indies took us a bit easy in the first Test. After all, they'd beaten us 4-1 in the one-day games, and seen our two main strike bowlers go home. I really think they do fear Craig McDermott. They rate him highly. I honestly think that their attitude once we had lost Craig was that that was the end of us. It showed on the first day in Barbados when they won the toss and came out playing shots from the opening ball against our inexperienced attack. It took them a day to wake up to it, and at that stage they were out for 195, and we were 2-91, and threatening. We never let go in that match: we found the extra ten per cent we had been looking for. To win that match in three days, and by ten wickets, after what we had been through was a genuinely outstanding achievement.

The end of the match sticks in my mind. I really wanted to hit the winning run, and in fact I hit three fours off Kenneth Benjamin's last over. But the winning run was a no-ball when he came around the wicket at me. At least I was on strike.

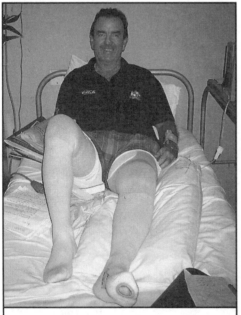

Bob Simpson laid up in Barbados hospital.

I promptly grabbed the three stumps, and I've got one of them still safely tucked away — one from there and one from Jamaica. I gave one to Jimmy Adams who had asked me before the last ball was bowled if he could have one, and the other to Glenn McGrath, the man of the match and a bowler who should be a great asset for Australian teams for years to come. Slats had less luck than I did as the crowd managed to pinch the stumps from his end. The Aussie supporters in the crowd were great on that last day in Barbados. I can still see them out the front of the dressing room, singing 'Waltzing Matilda' and 'Advance Australia Fair' and waving the flag. The Aussie tourists were unbelievably keen. They'd come down to our training sessions on the old Police Ground, and I'd invite them to field. I'm sure they were tickled pink to be there, but it helped us too. We had our own little slice of Australia right there in the West Indies.

The last batsman is dismissed. Australia has won the Frank Worrell Trophy and the celebrations are about to begin.

The rain had the final say in the second Test, but the quality of our comeback after they had been 3-186, chasing our modest total of 216, was highly encouraging. Without rain I think we would have stretched them right out on the last day. A last-innings 250 target would have been very tough for them, I think.

The key to the Trinidad Test on that slow, under-prepared strip was just one session of play. It was level-pegging until then, with some fine bowling and fielding on our part after we'd got out only 128 to keep them down to 136. But the morning of the third day killed us when we lost eight wickets for hardly any. In two hours, the game was gone. I'm sure at that point plenty of people were ready to write us off again. 'Ambrose is back, Walsh is back . . . blah, blah, blah.'

The funny thing, after the way it all turned out, is that I believed at the start of the tour that Barbados and Jamaica would be the two grounds where the West Indies were most dangerous to us. History now records that we won them both! The fourth Test in Jamaica was an occasion that will live in the memories of all of us who played in it. Steve Waugh's 200 was an amazing innings, a truly great innings. For him to ever play a better one in Test cricket would have to be something very special indeed. He deserved his Man of the Match, and he deserved his Man of the Series. Tug just had a wonderful campaign. He copped some flak over the Brian Lara catch in the first Test in Barbados, but turned it to his advantage. He channelled his aggression the right way, and used it against them – not verbally, and not off the field, but *on* the field where it counted. In my view he's the best batsman in the world at the moment. He's a great pal of mine, and maybe that makes me a bit biased, but if making runs in Test cricket is what makes you a good batsmen then he's the best. He may not always *look* the best — I think that Brian Lara and Sachin Tendulkar may look a bit more impressive at times — but Steve is the most determined of them all, the hardest man to get out in Test cricket.

To win in Jamaica by an innings and 53 runs after *again* losing the toss on a very good wicket was a sign that we are now a very good cricket team, a better one than we were. Sabina Park, Jamaica, 1995, will be remembered as an epic Australian Test match win. It will be remembered because not only did it represent the first victory by an innings over the West Indies in more than a decade, but that it broke a drought of nineteen years in the winning of the Frank Worrell Trophy. To win, we had to fight back from a potentially destabilising loss in Trinidad, and we did it.

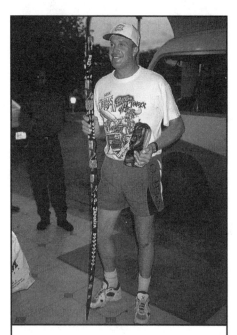

Carl Rackemann outside the team hotel on the rest day in the fourth Test.

Richie Richardson made some comments after the Test which attracted a great deal of media interest. He said in so many words that we were the weakest Australian side he had played against. It was very disappointing and created a wide perception that Richie was both a bad loser and a bad sport. I don't believe that he could be classified

as either. I know him better than that. I think I know what he meant to say –
but it didn't come out right. I think he looked at our side at the start of the
Test series, saw no Craig McDermott, saw no Damien Fleming, didn't see the
big names that he'd been used to seeing in past Aussie bowling lineups. He
knew the wickets probably weren't going to suit Shane Warne too much and
I'm sure that deep down he really thought that they were going to score lots of
runs. As it turned out 265 was their biggest score of the series.

In what he said I think Richie just showed inexperience. He was a guy who
had played Test cricket for eleven or twelve years and had never played in a
series-losing side. I think that what he said afterwards just showed that he wasn't
used to losing. What he most likely meant was that this was the worst Australian
side, *on paper*, that he had played against. Maybe he wasn't so far off the mark . . .
on paper. I'm sure he didn't mean it to sound the way it did – that he was bitter, a
sore loser, all that sort of thing. If it had been some other cricketers you might
have read something else into it. But not Richie. He probably learned
something from the loss . . . and he probably had a hard lesson driven home by
the things he said afterwards.

Essentially I think that our winning the series was good for cricket. The fact
that someone has knocked the West Indies off after fifteen years of dominance
has got to be healthy for everyone. Suddenly there's a new force at the top of
world cricket, and everyone can take
heart from that. I think we all know one
thing though – that the West Indies are
going to bounce back as hard as they
can.

The debate is raging at the moment
whether or not we are entitled to be
called 'world champions'. I believe we
are. Maybe there are all sorts of ways of
looking at it. To me the only way to
work it out is to judge it like a world
boxing title. If you beat the best on
their home turf, under their
conditions, then you're entitled to be
called the 'best'. What with different
seasons around the world, different
grounds and different conditions, it's
hard to say at any given moment who is
the best. But if you beat the team rated
the best, and on their home track, then
you put in a pretty fair claim. If Pakistan
come to Australia this year and happen
to knock us off in a home series, then

SHAUN BOTTERILL/ALLSPORT•AUSTRALIAN PICTURE LIBRARY

*Mark Waugh: together with brother
Steve he put on 231 for the fourth wicket
in the first innings, of the fourth Test,
setting up Australia's win.*

they're entitled to grab the mantle of 'world champions'. Meanwhile, we'll wear it with pride.

The aftermath of the fourth Test had its share of disappointments, for all the joy that existed in the Australian camp. As soon as I walked off the field I was thinking about what I wanted to say when I was handed the Frank Worrell Trophy. But the post-match ceremony was a disappointment. The PA system was on the blink, and a speech that meant a lot to me in representing Australia was probably heard by hardly anyone at the ground. There was a heap of noise. The Aussie supporters were singing and carrying on, and that was fair enough. But I was disappointed that people in the crowd who had come along to support cricket and the series didn't hear a word of it.

The two Waughs after each scored 100s in the fourth Test.

Prior to the match Jim Maxwell had played an audio tape for me of the ceremony that followed the great Australia-West Indies series of 1961. It started with Sir Donald Bradman presenting the trophy to Australia's captain Richie Benaud. Benaud spoke and then Frank (later Sir Frank) Worrell replied. I thought about that when I went up to try and get my own words right. I was very disappointed with what happened. Apart from the other things I wanted to say, I was keen to express my own and the team's appreciation of the supporters who had followed us to the West Indies. I learned later that my words were picked up by the television mikes and relayed back home, so I was happy about that at least.

I can tell you that the party that followed what we achieved at Sabina Park was a BIG one. Not that there was anything too special about it, really. We just sat around with big smiles on our faces, had a few beers and enjoyed the feeling. At the moment we're six or seven days into the Bermuda 'leg' and only now am I coming back down to earth. Only now am I starting to think about getting back home, and some more normal things. It's just been one long party since Sabina Park. I'm pleased that Allan Border was there to enjoy the victory, and to be part of the celebrations. He was so much a part of this team. I am privileged and proud to be captain of such a team; I hope I've made a contribution to its success, and no-one would question the fact that AB did in all the years he was at the helm.

I'm starting to think of the whole thing as the 'Comeback Tour'. Because that's what it was — coming back after the disappointment of the one-dayers, after losing our two main quicks, coming back, it seemed, whenever some adversity was upon us. *Team* was the operative word. We worked together, helped each other out as much as we could and talked about what we were doing wrong, and what we had to do to make it right. The communication within the side was just great.

It's funny the things that stick in your mind. The trip back to our hotel after the last day at Sabina Park was just memorable. We were singing the Cold Chisel songs 'Ke San' and 'Bow River', and throwing in our own lyrics. When we pulled up outside the Pegasus Hotel we were still singing, and the bellboys and all the staff were in the foyer, and clapped us in. It was after nine before I finally checked into the hotel that night. I figured I'd better do it then because I mightn't be capable later on. Chances were we were all going to get drunk . . . and I reckoned we deserved to.

I sat there alone in my room for a time that night. The light was flashing madly on the telephone, and every couple of minutes it would ring. I just let it ring. There were fifty or sixty faxes under my door, and downstairs the machine was buzzing away endlessly. I had mixed feelings, most of them overwhelming and very hard for me to put into words. I thought of Allan Border who

Let the celebrations begin. Michael Slater, Glenn McGrath and Justin Langer getting into party mode. In the background Allan Border and Carl Rackemann enjoy the taste of victory.

was here with us for the celebrations and who, for all the hard work and all the talent he put into it, had never had his hands on the Frank Worrell Trophy. Tonight, at least, he can do that. AB's congratulations meant more to me than a thousand back-slaps from well-wishers. He wanted us to win this series as much as *we* wanted to win it . . . and he wasn't even playing.

Nights like that one make it all worthwhile. They go a long way towards making up for the times of loneliness and the sacrifice. They help make up for the times when all you want to do is be with your family. People say it's a great and glamorous lifestyle, being an Australian Test cricketer. And it can be at times. But you give up some things, too. There are plenty of nights when you think about your kids, growing up at home without you. I live a life which is not exactly normal, for all its so-called 'glamour' and attractions. Some days and nights on tour I hanker for a 'normal' life. One day I guess I'll have it. But in room whatever it was in the Pegasus Hotel, Jamaica, on a night in May, I guess I wouldn't have changed a single thing.

We had flown across the world to the Caribbean islands to play cricket against the West Indies.

And we had won.

PRIME MINISTER

CANBERRA

4 MAY 1995

Mr Mark Taylor
Captain
Australian Cricket Team

Dear Mark

Congratulations on a magnificent and historic series victory in the West Indies.

In winning the Sir Frank Worrell Trophy on West Indies soil, the Australian team has achieved the ultimate in contemporary cricket. The Australian effort had brilliant individual performances with bat and ball but, above all, it was a superb team achievement. This reflects tremendous credit on your leadership, on and off the field.

Please pass on my congratulations and best wishes to every team member.

All Australians are very proud of you today.

Yours sincerely

P J KEATING

Just one of the many faxes received by Mark and the team.

Chapter 9

FINAL
OVERS

BOUNCER WARS

Before our last Test against the West Indies I made a comment to Trent Bouts of *The Australian* about one of our game's laws that I don't think is working. It's called Experimental Law 42.8, which says that a bowler can bowl only two bouncers in any one over, and that to qualify as a bouncer the ball has to bounce over the batsman's head. I'm sure the experimental law was introduced with the best intentions, to assist umpires in deciding what is unfair — or intimidatory — bowling to dismiss a batsman. The experimental law is to be used in conjuction with the old Law 42.8 which decreed that a bowler was not allowed to use intimidation as a method of getting a batsman out. It was a very subjective rule, for sure, and placed a heavy burden on umpires who had to determine the bowler's intention. But in my book, the old law 42.8 was the best way to ascertain intimidation. Using the experimental law 42.8 a bowler can now bowl up to six short balls an over, providing that only two pass over the shoulder of the batsman. I believe that as a result a quality fast bowler can intimidate a batsman without bowling so-called 'bouncers'. I'm not pointing the finger at any particular bowler or team because I believe that all teams — Australia included — are at times guilty of intimidatory bowling. What I would like to do is to see umpires enforce the original law 42.8 — and rid the game of intimidatory bowling. Perhaps that represents an extra burden on umpires, but it's the only logical answer.

SPIRIT OF THE GAME

Another problem holding cricket back in the 1990s is the inconsistency in the rules of the game. There is definitely a crying need to standardise the game's regulations. For instance, during Tests in some countries the second new ball is taken after 75 overs; in others it is taken after 85 overs. I believe a uniform figure should be agreed upon. In one-day matches there are a number of different formulae for determining the target score in games interrupted by rain. Again, I believe a common formula is the answer — making the game easier for both players and spectators.

Often, though, when looking at some of the problems that beset our sport, it comes down to captains upholding the spirit of the game. If a game is played hard and fair, there's no problem. But when teams start exploiting loopholes in the rule book to take what I feel is an unfair advantage over their rivals then trouble begins. Umpires shouldn't have to be policemen: their ideal role is to make the game flow. Captains and players can help in this regard and if we all approach the game the way it should be, then you'll have a good game of cricket on your hands.

OUR HECTIC SCHEDULE

International cricketers these days play up to nine months of every year. It's a gruelling and demanding schedule, hard work year in, year out, all over the world. There's nothing we can do about a pressing itinerary — like last year's, when we played Pakistan and Sri Lanka away, England at home, New Zealand away and the Windies in the Caribbean — but we Australians are trying to lighten the load in other ways. We've changed our training schedule — because we play more often our match fitness will always be okay and scaled training down. Certainly we do less on the training paddock than past sides. While we all know you have to train enough to be able to bat, bowl, field and keep going at top pace for six hours a day, five days in a row, we are mixing the hard yakka with lots of wind-down leisure activities to ensure we don't get stale, fatigued and burned out.

For instance, at the beginning of last season, Heals, Bob Simpson and I sat down and mapped out our year. We decided that to last the season and remain at our physical and mental peak we would take training a bit easy in Sri Lanka and New Zealand — no net sessions, just a bit of aerobics and water aerobics — but pour on the work during the Pakistan, England and West Indies series. The proof of our tactics is in the pudding. Right now, as I write this, we have just beaten the West Indies in the Caribbean where we played the very best cricket of the season. That we were able to save the best till last is a result of the way we paced ourselves through the year.

THAT ANSETT AD

Now that was a bit of fun. Steve Waugh and me on the rub-down bench in the changerooms, with a big masseur. Before Steve Waugh and I shot it at North Sydney Oval, I sat down for an hour and a half with a guy named Frank who was teaching me the basics of Cantonese. I repeated my lines to him and he made sure I sounded authentic. The ad took half a day to shoot. Everywhere I go now, people say to me, 'Gay Pil Gar!' (The punch to the ad.)

Last year after a one-day game in Melbourne, John 'Strop' Cornell, the bloke who produced *Crocodile Dundee* with Paul Hogan, came up to me in the dressing room and said, 'That Ansett ad you did was a beauty.'

I thought he was taking the mickey and I said, 'Oh, yeah, righto, John.'

He said, 'No, no, I'm serious. I think you cricketers have great scripts.'

I thought, 'Great script!. . . I talked Cantonese all the way through.' It was a lot of fun, and a bit of light relief in a tough season. I'd do another one tomorrow if the job was offered.

JUGGLING RESPONSIBILITIES

For me the hardest thing about being captain of Australia is finding time to honour my many cricket commitments, and be a good husband and father. The demands are endless. When we returned from the Windies tour we were bone-tired, and all we wanted to do was bunker down with our families, but we were told that they were planning a motorcade in Sydney and Melbourne. Now that would have been great and a fun day, but for me it would have been just one more day away from Judi, William and Jack. When I got home, Jack was three months old, but I'd spent only a fortnight with him. William had his third birthday on 16 May, but we didn't arrive home from the Caribbean until three days later, so I wasn't there to help him blow out the candles on his birthday cake. I haven't seen as much of him as I'd have liked, nor he of me.

Luckily I have a wonderful wife who understands my job and my responsibilities. She knows that to play at the highest level of sport at times you have to put that sport before family, and that although I would rather be home with the kids I must be touring, playing, training, attending meetings or fulfilling media obligations. As I've said, it comes with the job of being Australian skipper. We constantly talk about the pressures and that helps us to survive them, knowing they will not last forever. It's a bit like the way I operate as skipper. If I have a problem with a player I sit down and talk the problem through. The same thing happens with Judi. She tells me what she's thinking and I do the same to her.

ON CAPTAINCY

My views on captaincy didn't really change in the 1994-95 season. What happened tended to reinforce my thinking. I'm confident with the captaincy now, and so I should be. I have a talented and united team behind me and we ended the season unofficial world champions after beating the Windies convincingly. I suppose I see myself as a manager of my men. I look after them and their interests.

My players know I am there for them. It is in my interest to be. I know that if Shane Warne is to perform at his top on the pitch he has to feel right within himself, not just about cricket but in his whole life. Likewise with the other batsmen and bowlers. They may still score a duck and take no wickets for a hundred, but they'll be giving their best and that's all any skipper can expect. And, of course, even when some fail, if the team is confident and happy others will succeed. It stands to reason. I think I have the players' respect. They are comfortable with me at the helm, they know me and the way I operate.

There's no doubt that being captain has changed the way I bat. I believe I must set an example through my batting to be positive and take the fight to the opposition, to inspire my men. It's no longer a question of simply accumulating runs. I need to be aggressive, as in the Newcastle game against England when I took their bowlers on and belted them around. The other players followed suit and the Englishmen were on the back foot for the rest of the tour. Likewise, I made a deliberate effort in the West Indies to be very positive, to show the other players that we could beat those blokes. A few times I got out hooking and some critics said I should cut the hook out of my repertoire, but they missed the point. I was attacking the bowling. The journalist Mike Coward wrote an article that I thought was right on the ball because he knew exactly what I was up to. He said that I was hooking to set a pattern of attacking their ferocious fast bowlers and meeting them head-on. Steve Waugh made the same statement, but in a totally different way. Steve didn't play a hook shot all season, but he made his point against Ambrose and Walsh by standing his ground and taking quite a few on his body while scoring a mountain of runs, especially that double century in the last Test. At the end of the series the Windies knew he wasn't afraid to challenge them with the bat or ball.

Finally on batting, I guess I would like to have a few more big scores to my name. I've only made one Test hundred as skipper, and that was against England in the Sydney Test. All the same, I think I've played reasonably well and I'm confident of getting some big scores next year.

WHERE DO WE GO FROM HERE?

When I took over the captaincy from Allan Border we were in magnificent shape. AB had done a splendid job and gave me a wonderful basis to work with. Today, after a year in charge, I think we are in even better shape, with a genuine opportunity to achieve greatness as a team. Having beaten the West Indies we've at last got rid of the hoodoo they had on us. We've proved we can be competitive against the Pakistanis in Pakistan, which some say is the hardest tour in international cricket. Winning away from home is important. We expect to win on the other team's turf as well as our own and that's a sign of a great side.

But greatness does not come easily. We have to knuckle down and get physically and mentally right for the challenges ahead. Being unofficial world champs is a double-edged sword. On the one hand, our standing can intimidate other teams, but it can also make them keener to knock us off. There will be no such thing as an easy series for us from now on.

I hope that with each year I captain my country — whether my incumbency lasts one year, two years or longer — that the experience will remain as exciting and rewarding as it has been in my first year. 1994-95 has been a season to remember.

Postscript
THE BOYS OF WINTER

It seemed much to the relief of Sydney folk when Mark Taylor and his men gatecrashed the football season of 1995 in a belated celebration of the glorious achievements of the West Indies campaign. The ticker tape parade through the deep canyons of downtown Sydney was, like a Test match checked by an 11am cloudburst, a little slow off the mark. The date was June 29, winter had thoroughly arrived and the sunny days in the Caribbean seemed long ago and far away. The sound of the steel drums were faint by then, and there was a wintry edge to the morning. But it was special, all the same. The football season was in ruins, thanks to the astonishing News Limited Super League raid and its aftermath. Sydney's workers, gathered at the kerbsides seemed happy, relieved almost, to briefly get back to something finer and simpler — and the reception they gave Australia's cricketers as the cavalcade twisted and turned through the streets was warm and enthusiastic. Several times the happy progress was halted by well-wishers and autograph hunters.

'It was very special for all of us,' said the skipper. 'We have been home a while — but all the same it was a genuine homecoming. The tour was a fair way behind us by then, and the crowd numbers were down a little on what they had been in 1989 when we brought back the Ashes from England. But the warmth of the greeting we were given and the interest in the team, I know, touched everyone in the side. It was certainly special for me — to get the chance to address the crowd from the Town Hall . . . then again in Martin Place. And then to lunch in Parliament House. It provided a *completeness* to what we had achieved on tour. We were home, with the Trophy, and the people were there to share it all with us. It was a day I will remember . . . at the end of such a year. I was very, very proud.'

Numerically, it was not a 'complete' morning. Five of the team were missing — Mark Waugh, Paul Reiffel and Carl Rackermann playing away, in England plus Rickie Ponting and Justin Langer, in camp in Brisbane, preparing to leave with the Australian A team for Britain. *The Sydney Morning Herald's* John Huxley profiled the event this way:

An amazed Tim May was mobbed by screaming schoolgirls. David Boon found himself dodging bunting rather than bouncers. And super-spinner Shane 'Hollywood' Warne signed autographs until his fabled 'golden' arm ached. But the biggest cheer of all was awarded to 'Captain Loquacious' Mark Taylor and his NSW teammate Steve Waugh, as Sydneysiders yesterday belatedly welcomed home Australia's cricketers yesterday from their historic, triumphant tour of the West Indies.

The Sydney Morning Herald's columnist Jeff Wells observed:

The best thing about Thursday was that it was a rare example of real contact between the players, who are necessarily cocooned by their sport, and the public. For one day they were no longer untouchables. For a change, we felt we knew them.

The Frank Worrell Trophy was never far from skipper Taylor's grasp. 'We'd like to hang onto this for quite a while . . . and make them suffer as we did', he told the crowd.

It had been quite a year. Ahead lay some family time, some getting ready time, Coach Bob Simpson had pencilled in September for the beginning of training. In November, the Pakistanis would arrive, with their challenge. It was soon enough.

But for the day, a cricket team, a crowd and a proud captain could forget for a while the hard graft. Today was about the sweet fruits of a breathtaking victory. 'Your support meant the world to us.' Mark Taylor told the crowd. And down the long, narrow streets of Sydney, the cheers rang out . . .

THE STORY IN STATS

First Class Career of
TAYLOR, Mark Anthony

Debut — 1985/86 New South Wales v Tasmania, Hobart (TCA)

Season	Country	M	Inn	N.O.	Runs	H.S.	50	100	Avrge	Ct	Runs	Wkts	Avrge	Best
1985/86		12	20	1	937	118	5	2	49.32	16	-	-	-	-
1985/86	Zimbabwe	2	4	-	46	23	-	-	11.50	2	-	-	-	-
1986/87		11	20	1	765	106	4	1	40.26	10	1	-	-	-
1987/88	Zimbabwe	2	3	-	71	44	-	-	23.67	-			-	-
1987/88		10	16	-	439	144	2	1	25.50	16			-	-
1988/89		14	26	1	1241	152	7	3	49.64	22	-	-	-	-
1989	England	17	30	1	1669	219	10	3	57.55	23	-	-	-	-
1989/90		11	19	1	1176	199	5	5	65.33	15	-	-	-	-
1989/90	New Zealand	1	2	-	9	5	-	-	4.50	2	-	-	-	-
1989/90		1	2	-	227	127	-	2	113.50	-	-	-	-	-
1990/91		8	14	1	495	183	3	1	38.08	13	-	-	-	-
1990/91	West Indies	10	14	-	777	144	5	3	55.50	6	-	-	-	-
1991/92	Zimbabwe	2	3	1	86	41	-	-	43.00	6	-	-	-	-
1991/92		14	24	1	925	158	7	2	40.22	75	1	-	-	-
1992/93	Sri Lanka	4	7	-	161	43	-	-	23.00	2	-	-	-	-
1992/93		8	15	1	530	102	1	2	37.86	8	9	-	-	-
1992/93	New Zealand	4	6	-	193	82	2	-	32.17	12	18	-	-	-
1993	England	15	25	2	972	124	4	3	42.26	25	31	1	31.00	1/4
1993/94		10	16	1	763	170	4	2	50.87	15	-	-	-	-
1993/94	South Africa	5	10	-	373	75	4	-	37.30	4	-	-	-	-
1994/95	Pakistan	4	7	1	111	69	1	-	18.50	4	11	1	11.00	1/11
1994/95		8	15	-	751	150	4	2	50.07	12	-	-	-	-
1994/95	West Indies	7	10	1	222	62	2	-	24.67	11	-	-	-	-
Total		180	310	14	12959	219	70	32	43.78	249	68	2	34.00	1/4
Test Cricket		66	119	8	5005	219	30	13	45.09	93	26	1	26.00	1/11
Sheffield Shield		65	112	3	4921	199	24	13	45.15	93	11	-	-	-
Domestic Limited Overs		24	24	-	790	84	8	-	32.92	15	3	-	-	-
Interna' Limited Overs		79	76	1	2411	97	21	-	32.15	43	-	-	-	-
World Series		35	34	-	1091	81	8	-	32.09	42				

Team	M	Inn	N.O	Runs	H.S	50	100	Avrge	Ct	Runs	Wkts	Avrge	Best
AUSTRALIA	66	119	8	5005	219	30	13	45.09	93	26	1	26.00	1/11
Australia XI	36	56	3	2204	141	13	4	41.58	51	31	1	31.00	1/4
New South Wales	78	135	3	5750	199	27	15	43.56	105	11	-	-	-

Highest Score: 219 AUSTRALIA v ENGLAND, Nottingham, 1989

100s	Team	Opponent	Venue	Season
119	New South Wales	South Australia	Sydney	1985/86
100	New South Wales	South Australia	Adelaide	1985/86
186	New South Wales	South Australia	Sydney	1986/87
144	New South Wales	Tasmania	Sydney	1987/88
107	New South Wales	Western Australia	Perth	1988/89
152	New South Wales	Western Australia	Perth	1988/89
132	New South Wales	Queensland	Sydney	1988/89
136	AUSTRALIA	ENGLAND	Leeds	1989
141	Australian XI	Gloucestershire	Bristol	1989
219	AUSTRALIA	ENGLAND	Nottingham	1989
199	New South Wales	South Australia	Adelaide	1989/90
164	AUSTRALIA	SRI LANKA	Brisbane	1989/90
108	AUSTRALIA	SRI LANKA	Hobart	1989/90
101	AUSTRALIA	PAKISTAN	Melbourne	1989/90
101	AUSTRALIA	PAKISTAN	Sydney	1989/90
127	New South Wales	Queensland	Sydney	1989/90
100	New South Wales	Queensland	Sydney	1989/90
183	New South Wales	Tasmania	Sydney	1990/91
101	Australian XI	West Indian Board XI	Bassetorre	1990/91
122	Australian XI	West Indies Under 23s	Kingstown	1990/91
144	AUSTRALIA	WEST INDIES	St John's	1990/91
100	AUSTRALIA	INDIA	Adelaide	1991/92
158	New South Wales	Victoria	Melbourne	1991/92
102	New South Wales	Victoria	Sydney	1992/93
101	New South Wales	WEST INDES	Sydney	1992/93
124	AUSTRALIA	ENGLAND	Manchester	1993
111	AUSTRALIA	ENGLAND	Lord's	1993
122	Australian XI	Lancashire	Manchester	1993
142	AUSTRALIA	NEW ZEALAND	Perth	1993/94
170	AUSTRALIA	SOUTH AFRICA	Melbourne	1993/94
150	New South Wales	England XI	Newcastle	1994/95
113	AUSTRALIA	ENGLAND	Sydney	1994/95

Best Bowling: 1/4 Australian XI v Kent, Canterbury, 1993

Test Career of TAYLOR, Mark Anthony

Debut: 1988/89 Australia v West Indies, Sydney

Season	Opponent	Venue	M	Inn	N.O.	Runs	H.S.	0s	50	100	Avrge	Ct
1988/89	West Indies	Australia	2	4	-	67	36	-	-	-	16.75	1
1989	England	England	6	11	1	839	219	-	5	2	83.90	5
1989/90	New Zealand	Australia	1	1	-	9	9	-	-	-	9.00	1
1989/90	Sri Lanka	Australia	2	4	-	304	164	-	-	2	76.00	3
1989/90	Pakistan	Australia	3	5	1	390	101*	-	3	2	97.50	8
1989/90	New Zealand	New Zealand	1	2	-	9	5	-	-	-	4.50	2
1990/91	England	Australia	5	10	1	213	67*	-	2	-	23.67	8
1990/91	West Indies	West Indies	5	9	-	441	144	1	4	1	49.00	3
1991/92	India	Australia	5	10	1	422	100	-	3	1	46.89	7
1992/93	Sri Lanka	Sri Lanka	3	6	-	148	43	-	-	-	24.67	1
1992/93	West Indies	Australia	4	8	1	170	46*	-	-	-	24.29	5
1992/93	New Zealand	New Zealand	3	4	-	148	82	-	2	-	37.00	7
1993	England	England	6	10	-	428	124	-	1	2	42.80	11
1993/94	New Zealand	Australia	3	4	1	286	142*	-	2	1	95.33	5
1993/94	South Africa	Australia	3	5	-	304	170	-	1	1	60.80	4
1993/94	South Africa	South Africa	2	4	-	97	70	-	1	-	24.25	2
1994/95	Pakistan	Pakistan	3	5	1	106	69	2	1	-	26.50	3
1994/95	England	Australia	5	10	-	471	113	-	4	1	47.10	7
1994/95	West Indies	West Indies	4	7	1	153	55	-	1	-	25.50	10
Total			66	119	8	5005	219	3	30	13	45.09	93

Opponents	M	Inn	N.O.	Runs	H.S.	0s	50	100	Avrge	Ct
ENGLAND	22	41	2	1951	219	-	12	5	50.03	31
INDIA	5	10	1	422	100	-	3	1	46.89	7
NEW ZEALAND	8	11	1	452	142*	-	4	1	45.20	15
PAKISTAN	6	10	2	496	101*	2	4	2	62.00	11
SRI LANKA	5	10	-	452	164	-	-	2	45.20	4
SOUTH AFRICA	5	9	-	401	170	-	2	1	44.56	6
WEST INDIES	15	28	2	831	144	1	5	1	31.96	19

	Inn	N.O.	Runs	H.S.	0s	50	100	Avrge	Ct
First Innings	41	-	1756	219	2	10	5	42.83	39
Second Innings	25	1	1156	101*	-	12	1	48.17	19
Third Innings	33	2	1470	164	1	4	6	47.42	17
Fourth Innings	20	5	623	113	-	4	1	41.53	18

* Denotes not out.

Venue	M	Inn	N.O.	Runs	H.S.	0s	50	100	Avrge	Ct
in Australia										
Adelaide	7	14	-	506	100	-	4	1	36.14	5
Brisbane	6	11	2	590	164	-	5	1	65.56	5
Hobart	2	3	-	158	108	-	-	1	52.67	6
Melbourne	6	11	-	545	170	-	3	2	49.55	14
Perth	5	9	1	325	142*	-	2	1	40.63	10
Sydney	7	13	2	512	113	-	1	2	46.55	9
in England										
Birmingham	2	4	-	117	51	-	1	-	29.25	3
Leeds	2	3	-	223	136	-	1	1	74.33	3
Lord's	2	3	-	200	111	-	1	1	66.67	2
Manchester	2	4	1	255	124	-	1	1	85.00	3
Nottingham	2	3	-	275	219	-	-	1	91.67	2
The Oval	2	4	-	197	71	-	2	-	49.25	3
in New Zealand										
Auckland	1	2	-	16	13	-	-	-	8.00	3
Christchurch	1	1	-	82	82	-	1	-	82.00	2
Wellington	2	3	-	59	50	-	1	-	19.67	4
in Pakistan										
Karachi	1	2	-	0	0	2	-	-	0.00	3
Lahore	1	1	-	32	32	-	-	-	32.00	-
Rawalpindi	1	2	1	74	69	-	1	-	74.00	-
in Sri Lanka										
Colombo PIS	1	2	-	41	26	-	-	-	20.50	-
Colombo SSC	1	2	-	85	43	-	-	-	42.50	-
Moratuwa	1	2	-	22	19	-	-	-	11.00	-
in South Africa										
Cape Town	1	2	-	84	70	-	1	-	42.00	2
Durban	1	2	-	13	12	-	-	-	6.50	-
in West Indies										
Bridgetown	2	4	1	173	76	-	2	-	57.67	5
Georgetown	1	2	-	15	15	1	-	-	7.50	-
Kingston	2	2	-	66	58	-	1	-	33.00	1
Port-of-Spain	2	4	-	95	61	-	1	-	23.75	3
St John's	2	4	-	245	144	-	1	1	61.25	4

Country	M	Inn	N.O.	Runs	H.S.	0s	50	100	Avrge	Ct
Australia	33	61	5	2636	170	-	15	8	47.07	49
England	12	21	1	1267	219	-	6	4	63.35	16
New Zealand	4	6	-	157	82	-	2	-	26.17	9
Pakistan	3	5	1	106	69	2	1	-	26.50	3
Sri Lanka	3	6	-	148	43	-	-	-	24.49	1
South Africa	2	4	-	97	70	-	1	-	24.25	2
West Indies	9	16	1	594	144	1	5	1	39.60	13

Batting Position	M	Inn	N.O.	Runs	H.S.	0s	50	100	Avrge	Ct
1/2	66	119	8	5005	219	3	30	13	45.09	93

Dismissals	M	Inn	No	Bwd	Cgt	LBW	Stp	Ro	HW	HB
	66	119	8	12	63	23	6	7	-	-

Highest Score: 219 AUSTRALIA v ENGLAND, Nottingham, 1989

100s	Team	Opponent	Venue	Season
136	AUSTRALIA	ENGLAND	Leeds	1989
219	AUSTRALIA	ENGLAND	Nottingham	1989
164	AUSTRALIA	SRI LANKA	Brisbane	1989/90
108	AUSTRALIA	SRI LANKA	Hobart	1989/90
101	AUSTRALIA	PAKISTAN	Melbourne	1989/90
101*	AUSTRALIA	PAKISTAN	Sydney	1989/90
144	AUSTRALIA	WEST INDIES	St John's	1990/91
100	AUSTRALIA	INDIA	Adelaide	1991/92
124	AUSTRALIA	ENGLAND	Manchester	1993
111	AUSTRALIA	ENGLAND	Lord's	1993
142*	AUSTRALIA	NEW ZEALAND	Perth	1993/94
170	AUSTRALIA	SOUTH AFRICA	Melbourne	1993/94
113	AUSTRALIA	ENGLAND	Sydney	1994/95

INNINGS BY INNINGS

Game	Inn	Date	Opp	Venue	Inn	Pos	H.O.	Fielder	Bowler	Runs	Ttl	Avrge

1988/89 in Australia

Game	Inn	Date	Opp	Venue	Inn	Pos	H.O.	Fielder	Bowler	Runs	Ttl	Avrge
1	1	10/01/1989	W.I	Sydney	2	2	BWD		Ambrose, CEL	25	25	25.00
1	2	26/01/1989	W.I	Sydney	4	1	CGT	Haynes, DL	Ambrose, CEL	3	28	14.00
2	3	03/02/1989	W.I	Adelaide	1	2	RO			3	31	10.33
2	4	03/02/1989	W.I	Adelaide	3	1	RO			36	67	16.75

1989 in England

Game	Inn	Date	Opp	Venue	Inn	Pos	H.O.	Fielder	Bowler	Runs	Ttl	Avrge
3	5	08/06/1989	ENG	Leeds	1	2	LBW		Foster, NA	136	203	40.60
3	6	08/06/1989	ENG	Leeds	3	1	CGT	Broad, BC	Pringle, DR	60	263	43.83
4	7	22/06/1989	ENG	Lord's	2	2	LBW		Foster, NA	62	325	46.43
4	8	22/06/1989	ENG	Lord's	4	1	CGT	Gooch, GA	Foster, NA	27	352	44.00
5	9	06/07/1989	ENG	Birmingham	1	2	STP	Russell, RC	Emburey, JE	43	395	43.89
5	10	06/07/1989	ENG	Birmingham	3	1	CGT	Botham, IT	Gooch, GA	51	446	44.60
6	11	27/07/1989	ENG	Manchester	2	1	STP	Russell, RC	Emburey, JE	85	531	48.27
6	12	27/07/1989	ENG	Manchester	4	2	N.O.			37	568	51.64
7	13	10/08/1989	ENG	Nottingham	1	2	GTP	Russell, RC	Cook, NGB	219	787	65.50
8	14	28/08/1989	ENG	The Oval	1	2	CGT	Russell, RC	Igglesden, AP	71	858	66.00
8	15	24/08/1989	ENG	The Oval	3	1	CGT	Russell, RC	Small, GC	48	906	64.71

1989/90 in Australia

Game	Inn	Date	Opp	Venue	Inn	Pos	H.O.	Fielder	Bowler	Runs	Ttl	Avrge
9	16	24/11/1989	N.Z	Perth	1	1	CGT	Wright, JG	Morrison, DK	9	915	61.00
10	17	08/12/1989	S.L	Brisbane	1	2	CGT	Wickramasinghe, AGD	Ramanayake,CPH	9	924	57.75
10	18	08/12/1989	S.L	Brisbane	3	1	LBW		Ramanayake,CPH	164	1088	64.00
11	19	16/12/1989	S.L	Hobart	1	2	CGT	Tillakaratne, HP	Ratnayake, RJ	23	1111	61.72
11	20	16/12/1989	S.L	Hobart	3	1	CGT	Gurusinha, AP	De Silva, PA	108	1219	64.16
12	21	12/01/1990	PAK	Melbourne	1	2	CGT	Aaqib Javed	Imran Khan	52	1271	63.65
12	22	12/01/1990	PAK	Melbourne	3	1	CGT	Aamir Malik	Tauseef Ahmed	101	1372	65.33
13	23	19/01/1990	PAK	Adelaide	2	2	LBW		Imran Khan	77	1449	65.86
13	24	19/01/1990	PAK	Adelaide	4	1	CGT	Saeed Anwar	Mushtaq Ahmed	59	1508	65.57
14	25	03/02/1990	PAK	Sydney	2	1	N.O.			101*	1609	69.96

(Dates represent starting date of each game)

1989/90 in New Zealand

15	26	15/03/1990	N.Z	Wellington	1	1	LBW		Morrison, DK	4	1613	67.21
15	27	15/03/1990	N.Z	Wellington	3	2	LBW		Hadlee, RJ	5	1618	64.72

1990/91 in Australia

16	28	23/11/1990	ENG	Brisbane	2	2	CGT	Lewis, CC	Fraser, ARC	10	1628	62.62
16	29	23/11/1990	ENG	Brisbane	4	1	N.O.			67*	1695	65.19
17	30	26/12/1990	ENG	Melbourne	2	2	CGT	Russell, RC	De Freitas, PAJ	61	1756	65.04
17	31	26/12/1990	ENG	Melbourne	4	1	CGT	Atherton, MA	Malcolm, DE	5	1761	62.09
18	32	04/01/1991	ENG	Sydney	1	2	CGT	Russell, RC	Malcolm, DE	11	1772	61.10
18	33	04/01/1991	ENG	Sydney	3	1	LBW		Hemmings, EE	19	1791	59.70
19	34	25/01/1991	ENG	Adelaide	1	2	RO			5	1796	57.94
19	35	25/01/1991	ENG	Adelaide	3	1	RO			4	1800	56.25
20	36	01/02/1991	ENG	Perth	2	2	CGT	Stewart, AJ	Malcolm, DE	12	1812	54.91
20	37	01/02/1991	ENG	Perth	4	1	CGT	Stewart, AJ	DeFreitas, PAJ	19	1831	53.85

1990/91 in West Indies

21	38	01/03/1991	W.I	Kingston	2	2	CGT	Hooper, CL	Patterson, BP	58	1889	53.97
22	39	23/03/1991	W.I	Georgetown	1	1	LBW		Patterson, DP	0	1889	52.47
22	40	23/03/1991	W.I	Georgetown	3	2	LBW		Ambrose, CEL	15	1904	51.46
23	41	05/04/1991	W.I	Port-of-Spain	1	2	CGT	Walsh, CA	Marshall, MD	61	1965	51.71
23	42	05/04/1991	W.I	Port-of-Spain	3	1	BWD		Patterson, BP	2	1967	50.44
24	43	19/04/1991	W.I	Bridgetown	2	1	LBW		Ambrose, CEL	26	1993	49.83
24	44	19/04/1991	W.I	Bridgetown	4	2	LBW		Marshall, MD	76	2069	50.46
25	45	27/04/1991	W.I	St John's	1	1	CGT	Dujon, PJL	Hooper, CL	59	2128	50.67
25	46	27/04/1991	W.I	St John's	3	2	C&B	Ambrose, CEL	Ambrose, CEL	144	2272	52.84

1991/92 in Australia

26	47	29/11/1991	IND	Brisbane	2	2	CGT	Vengsarkar, DB	Raju, SLV	94	2366	53.77
26	48	26/12/1991	IND	Brisbane	4	1	N.O.			35*	2401	54.57
27	49	26/12/1991	IND	Melbourne	2	2	CGT	Tendulkar, SR	Prabhakar, M	13	2414	53.64
27	50	26/12/1991	IND	Melbourne	4	1	STP	Moro, KS	Raju, SZV	60	2474	53.78
28	51	02/01/1992	IND	Sydney	1	2	CGT	Pandit, CS	Banarjes, S	56	2530	53.83
28	52	02/01/1992	IND	Sydney	3	1	CGT	Kapil Dev	Shastri, RJ	35	2565	53.44
29	53	25/01/1992	IND	Adelaide	1	2	BWD		Tendulkar, SR	11	2576	52.57
29	54	25/01/1992	IND	Adelaide	3	1	CGT	Raju, SLV	Kapil Dev	100	2676	53.52
30	55	01/02/1992	IND	Perth	1	1	CGT	Srikkanth, K	Kapil Dev	2	2678	52.51
30	56	01/02/1992	IND	Perth	3	1	LBW		Kapil Dev	16	2694	51.81

1992/93 in Sri Lanka

31	57	17/08/1992	S.L	Colombo SSC	1	1	LBW		Wick'singhe, GP	42	2736	51.62
31	58	17/08/1992	S.L	Colombo SSC	3	2	CGT	Gurusinha, AP	Anurasiri, GD	43	2779	51.46
32	59	28/08/1992	S.L	Colombo PIS	1	2	CGT	Jayasuriya, GT	Hathurusingha, UC	15	2794	50.80
32	60	28/08/1992	S.L	Colombo PIS	3	1	LBW		Hathurusingha, C	26	2820	50.36
33	61	08/09/1992	S.L	Moratuwa	1	2	CGT	Ranatunga, A	Anuragiri, SU	19	2839	49.81
33	62	08/09/1992	S.L	Moratuwa	3	1	CGT	Mahanama, RS	Liyanage, DK	3	2842	49.00

1992/93 in Australia

34	63	27/11/1992	W.I	Brisbane	1	1	CGT	Williams, D	Bishop, IR	7	2849	48.29
34	64	27/11/1992	W.I	Brisbane	3	2	CGT	Williams, D	Walsh, CA	34	2883	48.05
35	65	26/12/1992	W.I	Melbourne	1	2	CGT	Lara, BC	Walsh, CA	13	2896	47.48
35	66	26/12/1992	W.I	Melbourne	3	1	BWD		Bishop, IR	42	2938	47.39
36	67	02/01/1993	W.I	Sydney	1	2	CGT	Murray, JR	Bishop, IR	20	2958	46.95
36	68	02/01/1993	W.I	Sydney	3	1	N.O.			46*	3004	47.68
37	69	23/01/1993	W.I	Adelaide	2	1	CGT	Hooper, CL	Bishop, IR	1	3005	46.95
37	70	23/01/1993	W.I	Adelaide	4	2	CGT	Murray, JR	Benjamin, KCG	7	3012	46.34

1992/93 in New Zealand

38	71	25/02/1993	N.Z	Christchurch	1	2	CGT	Crowe, MD	Morrison, DK	82	3094	46.88
39	72	04/03/1993	N.Z	Wellington	2	1	RO			50	3144	46.93
40	73	12/03/1993	N.Z	Auckland	1	2	LBW		Morrison, DK	13	3157	46.43
40	74	12/03/1993	N.Z	Auckland	3	1	STP	Blain, TE	Patel, DN	3	3160	45.80

1993 in England

41	75	03/06/1993	ENG	Manchester	1	1	C&B	Such, PM	Such, PM	124	3284	46.91
41	76	03/06/1993	ENG	Manchester	3	2	LBW		Such, PM	9	3293	46.30
42	77	17/06/1993	ENG	Lord's	1	1	STP	Steward, AJ	Tufnell, PCR	111	3404	47.20
43	78	01/07/1993	ENG	Nottingham	2	2	CGT	Stewart, AJ	McCague, MJ	28	3432	47.01
43	79	01/07/1993	ENG	Nottingham	4	1	CGT	Atherton, MA	Such, PM	28	3460	46.76
44	80	22/07/1993	ENG	Leeds	1	2	LBW		Bicknell, MP	27	3487	46.49
45	81	05/08/1993	ENG	Birmingham	2	1	RO			19	3506	46.13
45	82	05/08/1993	ENG	Birmingham	4	2	CGT	Thorpe, GP	Such, PM	4	3510	45.58
46	83	19/08/1993	ENG	The Oval	2	1	CGT	Hussain, N	Malcolm, DE	70	3580	45.90
46	84	19/08/1993	ENG	The Oval	4	2	BWD		Watkin, SL	8	3588	45.42

1993/94 in Australia

47	85	12/11/1993	N.Z	Perth	1	1	BWD		Cairns, CL	64	3652	45.65
47	86	12/11/1993	N.Z	Perth	3	2	N.O			142*	3794	47.43
48	87	26/11/1993	N.Z	Hobart (BEL)	1	1	CGT	Jones, AH	Su'a, ML	27	3821	47.17
49	88	03/12/1993	N.Z	Brisbane	2	2	CGT	Pocock, BA	Doull, SB	53	3874	47.24
50	89	26/12/1993	SAF	Melbourne	1	1	BWD		Symcox, PL	170	4044	48.72
51	90	02/01/1994	SAF	Sydney	2	2	CGT	Richardson, DJ	Donald, AA	7	4051	48.23
51	91	02/01/1994	SAF	Sydney	4	1	CGT	Richardson, DJ	De Villiers, PS	27	4078	47.98
52	92	28/01/1994	SAF	Adelaide	1	1	BWD		Kirsten, G	62	4140	48.14
52	93	28/01/1994	SAF	Adelaide	3	2	BWD		Snell, RP	38	4178	48.02

1993/94 in South Africa

53	94	17/03/1994	SAF	Cape Town	2	2	CGT	Richardson, DJ	De Villiers, PS	70	4248	48.27
53	95	17/03/1994	SAF	Cape Town	4	1	BWD		Donald, AA	14	4262	47.89
54	96	25/03/1994	SAF	Durban	1	2	LBW		Donald, AA	1	4263	47.37
54	97	25/03/1994	SAF	Durban	3	1	LBW		De Villiers, PS	12	4275	46.98

1994/95 in Pakistan

55	98	28/09/1994	PAK	Karachi	1	2	C&B	Wasim Akram	Wasim Akram	0	4275	46.47
55	99	28/09/1994	PAK	Karachi	3	1	CGT	Rashid Latif	Waqar Younis	0	4275	45.97
56	100	05/10/1994	PAK	Rawalpindi	1	1	LBW		Mohsin Kamal	69	4344	46.21
56	101	05/10/1994	PAK	Rawalpindi	4	2	N.O			5*	4349	46.27
57	102	01/11/1994	PAK	Lahore	2	2	CGT	Saeed Anwar	Mushtaq Ahmed	32	4381	46.12

58	103	25/11/1994	ENG	Brisbane	1	2	RO	(Gough/Rhodes)		59	4440	46.25
58	104	25/11/1994	ENG	Brisbane	3	1	CGT	Stewart, AJ	Tufnell, PCR	58	4498	46.37
59	105	24/12/1994	ENG	Melbourne	1	2	LBW		DeFreitas, PAJ	9	4507	45.99
59	106	24/12/1994	ENG	Melbourne	3	1	LBW		Gough, D	19	4526	45.72
60	107	01/01/1995	ENG	Sydney	2	2	C&B	Gough, D	Gough, D	49	4575	45.75
60	108	01/01/1995	ENG	Sydney	4	1	BWD		Malcolm, DE	113	4688	46.42
61	109	26/01/1995	ENG	Adelaide	2	2	LBW		Lewis, CC	90	4778	46.84
61	110	26/01/1995	ENG	Adelaide	4	1	CGT	Thorpe, GD	Malcolm, DE	13	4791	46.51
62	111	03/02/1995	ENG	Perth	1	2	CGT	Rhodes, SJ	Lewis, CC	9	4800	46.15
62	112	03/02/1995	ENG	Perth	3	1	BWD		Fraser, ARC	52	4852	46.21

63	113	31/03/1995	W.I	Bridgetown	2	2	CGT	Hooper, CL	Benjamin, KCG	55	4907	46.29
63	114	31/03/1995	W.I	Bridgetown	4	1	N.O.			16*	4923	46.44
64	115	08/04/1995	W.I	St John's	1	2	CGT	Walsh, CA	Ambrose, CEL	37	4960	46.36
64	116	08/04/1995	W.I	St John's	3	1	CGT	Murray, JR	Walsh, CA	5	4965	45.97
65	117	21/04/1995	W.I	Port-of-Spain	1	1	CGT	Adams, JC	Ambrose, CEL	2	4967	45.57
65	118	21/04/1995	W.I	Port-of-Spain	3	2	CGT	Murray, JR	Benjamin, KCG	30	4997	45.43
66	119	29/04/1995	W.I	Kingston	2	1	CGT	Adams, JC	Walsh, CA	8	5005	45.09
66	120	29/04/1995	W.I	Kingston	4	2	N.O.			0	5005	45.09

Australia's Leading Test Run Scorers

Batsman	M	Inn	N.O.	Runs	H.S.	50's	100's	Avrge
AR Border	156	265	44	11174	205	63	27	50.56
DC Boon	101	181	20	7111	200	31	20	44.17
GS Chappell	88	151	19	7110	247*	31	24	53.86
DG Bradman	52	80	10	6996	334	13	26	99.94
RN Harvey	79	137	10	6149	205	24	21	48.42
KD Walters	75	125	14	5357	250	33	15	48.26
IM Chappell	76	136	10	5345	196	26	14	42.42
WM Lawry	68	123	12	5234	210	27	13	47.15
MA Taylor	66	119	8	5005	219	30	13	45.09
RB Simpson	62	111	7	4869	311	27	10	46.81

Australian Test Cricket Captains

Captain	Tests as captain	Eng	Ind	NZ	Pak	SAf	SL	WI	Won	Lost	Drawn	Tie	Won Toss
DW Gregory	3	3	-	-	-	-	-	-	2	1	-	-	2
WL Murdoch	16	16	-	-	-	-	-	-	5	7	4	-	7
TP Horan	2	2	-	-	-	-	-	-	-	2	-	-	1
HH Massie	1	1	-	-	-	-	-	-	1	-	-	-	1
JM Blackham	8	8	-	-	-	-	-	-	3	3	2	-	4
HJH Scott	3	3	-	-	-	-	-	-	-	3	-	-	1
PS McDonnell	6	6	-	-	-	-	-	-	1	5	-	-	4
G Giffen	4	4	-	-	-	-	-	-	2	2	-	-	3
GHS Trott	8	8	-	-	-	-	-	-	5	3	-	-	5
J Darling	21	18	-	-	-	3	-	-	7	4	10	-	7
H Trumble	2	2	-	-	-	-	-	-	2	-	-	-	1
MA Noble	15	15	-	-	-	-	-	-	8	5	2	-	11
C Hill	10	5	-	-	-	5	-	-	5	5	-	-	5
SE Gregory	6	3	-	-	-	3	-	-	2	1	3	-	1
WW Armstrong	10	10	-	-	-	-	-	-	8	-	2	-	4
HL Collins	11	8	-	-	-	3	-	-	5	2	4	-	7
W Bardsley	2	2	-	-	-	-	-	-	-	-	2	-	1
J Ryder	5	5	-	-	-	-	-	-	1	4	-	-	2
WM Woodfull	25	15	-	-	-	5	-	5	14	7	4	-	12
VY Richardson	5	-	-	-	-	5	-	-	4	-	1	-	1
DG Bradman	24	19	5	-	-	-	-	-	15	3	6	-	10
WA Brown	1	-	-	1	-	-	-	-	1	-	-	-	-
AL Hassett	24	10	-	-	-	10	-	4	14	4	6	-	18
AR Morris	2	1	-	-	-	-	-	1	-	2	-	-	2
IW Johnson	17	9	2	-	1	-	-	5	7	5	5	-	6
RR Lindwall	1	-	1	-	-	-	-	-	-	-	1	-	-
ID Craig	5	-	-	-	-	5	-	-	3	-	2	-	3
R Benaud	28	14	5	-	3	1	-	5	12	4	11	1	11
RN Harvey	1	1	-	-	-	-	-	-	1	-	-	-	-
RB Simpson	39	8	10	-	2	9	-	10	12	12	15	-	20
BC Booth	2	2	-	-	-	-	-	-	-	-	-	-	1
WM Lawry	26	10	7	-	-	4	-	5	9	8	9	-	7
BN Jarman	1	1	-	-	-	-	-	-	-	-	1	-	1
IM Chappell	30	16	-	6	3	-	-	5	15	5	10	-	17
GS Chappell	48	15	3	8	9	-	1	12	21	13	14	-	29
GN Yallop	7	6	-	-	1	-	-	-	1	6	-	-	6
KJ Hughes	28	6	6	-	9	-	-	7	4	13	11	-	13
AR Border	93	29	11	17	6	6	6	18	32	22	38	1	46
MA Taylor	12	5	-	-	3	-	-	4	5	3	4	-	3
Total	552	286	50	32	37	59	7	81	227	155	168	2	268

Australia Under Taylor 1994-95 In Pakistan, 1994

LIMITED OVERS SERIES at SSC Ground, Colombo, Pakistan
7 September 1994

AUSTRALIA		PAKISTAN	
M Taylor LBW B Akram	8	Saeed Anwar c McGrath b S Waugh	46
M Slater c Mutjaba b Akram	4	Aamir Sohail b McGrath	0
D Boon b Raza	19	Inzamam-ul-Haq St Healy b Warne	29
M Waugh st Latif b Mushtaq	23	Basit Ali c and b Warne	0
S Waugh c Latif b Mushtaq	1	Salim Malik c Taylor b S Waugh	22
M Bevan c Mushtaq b Salim	37	Rashid Latif c Taylor b S Waugh	7
I Healy not out	30	Wasim Akram b McGrath	16
S Warne b Akram	30	Akram Raza c Healy b McDermott	10
C McDermott not out	2	Waqar Younis c Slater b Warne	2
		Mushtaq Ahmed not out	2
		Asif Mutjaba not out	1
Sundries	25	Sundries	16
Total 7 for 179		Total 9 for 151	

Fall of Wickets: 11, 34, 47, 49, 85, 128, 174

Bowling: Wasim Akram 10-2-24-3, Waqar Younis 8-2-43-0
Mushtaq Ahmed 10-1-34-2, Akram Raza 10-1-26-1
Aamir Sohail 7-0-17-0, Salim Malik 5-0-19-1
Overs: 50

AUSTRALIA WON BY 28 RUNS

Fall of Wickets: 2, 77, 83, 94, 124, 129, 129, 147, 150

Bowling: C McDermott 10-2-21-1, G McGrath 10-3-25-2,
T May 10-0-53-0, S Warne 10-1-29-3, S Waugh 10-1-16-3
Overs: 50

LIMITED OVERS SERIES at Premadassa Int Stadium, Pakistan
10 September 1994

INDIA		AUSTRALIA	
M Prabhaka c Slater b Warne	20	M. Slater c and b Prabhakar	4
S Tendulkar b McDermott	110	M Taylor c Prabhakar b Kapil	26
N Sidhu c Boon b May	24	M Waugh b Chauhan	61
M Azharuddin c Healy b McDermott	31	D Boon b Chauhan	40
V Kambli not out	43	S Waugh b Prabhakar	22
Kapil Dev run out	4	M Bevan c Sidhu b Kumble	26
A Bedade run out	1	C McDermott c Kumble b Prabhakar	2
N Mongia c Healy b Warne	3	I Healy run out	15
A. Kumble b S. Waugh	1	S Warne b Raju	1
R Chauhan not out	2	T May not out	1
		G McGrath run out	1
Sundries	7	Sundries	16
Total 8 for 246		Total 215	

Fall of Wickets: 87, 129, 173, 211, 217, 218, 226, 237

Bowling: C McDermott 10-1-46-2, G McGrath, 6-0-41-0
S Warne 10-0-53-2, T May 10-0-35-1, S Waugh, 8-1-33-1
M Bevan 2-0-17-0, M Waugh 4-0-19-0
Overs: 50

INDIA WON BY 31 RUNS

Fall of Wickets: 22, 56, 123, 143, 181, 183, 209, 212, 213, 215

Bowling: M Prabhakar 8-0-34-3, Kapil Dev 8-1-44-1,
Raju 9.4-0-38-1, A Kumble 9-0-31-1, R Chauhan 10-0-41-2
S Tendulkar 3-0-15-0
Overs: 47.4

LIMITED OVERS TOURNAMENT at Saravanamuttu Stadium, Colombo, Sri Lanka
13 September 1994

AUSTRALIA		SRI LANKA	
M Taylor c De Silva b Kalpage	41	R Mahanama b Warne	20
M Slater run out	24	S Jayasuriya c Taylor b Angel	0
M Waugh st Dassanayake b Jayasuriya	24	A De Silva st Healy b Warne	33
J Langer c Wickremasinghe b Kalpage	9	A Ranatunga lbw b S Waugh	59
S Waugh c Dassanayake b Jayasuriya	30	H Tillekaratne not out	29
M Bevan not out	47	R Kalpage not out	9
I. Healy run out	28		
G Robertson not out	5		
Sundries	17	Sundries	14
Total 6 for 225		Total 4 for 164	

Fall of Wickets: 61, 90, 100, 116, 144, 204

Bowling: P Wickremasinghe 7-0-29-0, C Vaas 9-2-26-0,
A Ranatunga 2-0-14-0, R Kalpage 9-0-42-2,
K Dharmasena 10-1-45-0, S Jayasuriya, 10-0-42-2
A De Silva 3-0-16-0

Overs: 50

SRI LANKA WON CHASING A RAIN REDUCED TARGET OF 163

Fall of Wickets: 4, 48, 102, 141

Bowling: J Angel 7-1-29-1, D Fleming, 6.4-0-42-0
S Warne 8-0-27-2, S Waugh 6-0-32-1,
G Robertson 7-0-24-0

Overs: 34.4

TEST SERIES AUSTRALIA -V- PAKISTAN

FIRST TEST at National Stadium, Karachi
28, 29, 30 September, 1, 2 October 1994

AUSTRALIA — FIRST INNINGS		PAKISTAN — FIRST INNINGS	
M Slater lbw b Akram	36	Saeed Anwar c M Waugh b May	85
M Taylor c and b Akram	0	Aamir Sohail c Bevan b Warne	36
D Boon b Mushtaq	19	Zahid Fazal c Boon b May	27
M Waugh c Zahid b Mushtaq	20	Salim Malik lbw b Angel	26
M Bevan c Sohail b Mushtaq	82	Basit Ali c Bevan b McGrath	0
S Waugh b Waqar	73	Inzamam Ul Haq c Taylor b Warne	9
I Healy c Latif b Waqar	57	Rashid Latif c Taylor b Warne	2
S Warne c Latif b Sohail	22	Wasim Akram c Healy b Angel	39
J Angel b Akram	5	Akram Raza b McGrath	13
T May not out	1	Waqar Younis c Healy b Angel	6
G McGrath b Waqar	0	Mushtaq Ahmed not out	2
Sundries	22	Sundries	11
Total 337		Total 256	

Fall of Wickets: 12, 41, 75, 95, 216, 281, 325, 335, 335, 337

Bowling: Wasim Akram 25-4-75-3, Waqar Younis, 19.2-2-75-3
Mushtaq Ahmed 24-2-97-3, Akram Raza 14-1-50-0,
Aamir Sohail 5-0-19-1, Salim Malik 1-0-7-0

Fall of Wickets: 90, 153, 154, 157, 175, 181, 200,
234, 253, 256

Bowling: G McGrath 25-6-70-2, J Angel 13.1-0-
54-3, T May 20-5-55-2, S Warne 27-10-61-3,
S Waugh 2-0-9-0

AUSTRALIA — SECOND INNINGS		PAKISTAN — SECOND INNINGS	
M Taylor c Latif b Waqar	0	Saeed Anwar c and b Angel	77
M Slater lbw b Mushtaq	23	Aamir Sohail run out	34
D Boon not out	114	Zahib Fazal c Boon b Warne	3
M Waugh b Waqar	61	Salim Malik c Taylor b Angel	43
M Bevan b Akram	0	Akram Raza lbw b Warne	2
S Waugh lbw b Akram	0	Basit Ali lbw b Warne	12
I Healy c Latif b Akram	8	Wasim Akram c and b Warne	4
S Warne lbw b Waqar	0	Inzamam-Ul-Haq not out	58
J Angel c Latif b Akram	8	Rashid Latif lbw b S Waugh	35
T May b Akram	1	Waqar Younis c Healy b Warne	7
G McGrath b Waqar	1	Mushtaq Ahmed not out	20
Sundries	16	Sundries	20
Total	232	Total 9 for	315

Fall of Wickets: 1, 49, 171, 174, 174, 213, 218, 227, 229, 232
Bowling: Wasim Akram 22-3-63-5,
Waqar Younis 18-2-69-4, Mushtaq Ahmed 21-3-51-1,
Akram Raza 10-1-19-0, Aamir Sohail 7-0-19-0

Fall of Wickets: 45, 64, 148, 157, 174, 179, 184, 236, 258
Bowling: G McGrath 6-2-18-0, J Angel 28-8-92-2, S Waugh 15-3-28-1, S Warne 36.1-12-89-5, T May 18-4-67-0, M Waugh 3-1-4-0

PAKISTAN WON BY 1 WICKET

SECOND TEST at Pindi Stadium, Rawalpindi
5, 6, 7, 8, 9 October 1994

AUSTRALIA — FIRST INNINGS		PAKISTAN — FIRST INNINGS	
M Taylor lbw b Kamal	69	Saeed Anwar c S Waugh b McDermott	15
M Slater c Inzamam b Kamal	110	Aamir Sohail b Fleming	80
D Boon b Mushtaq	4	Zahid Fazal b Fleming	10
M Waugh c Sohail b Kamal	68	Salim Malik b McDermott	33
M Bevan lbw b Waqar	70	Aamir Malik lbw b McDermott	11
S Waugh b Waqar	98	Inzamam-Ul-Haq lbw b Warne	14
I Healy c Kamal b Sohail	58	Rashid Latif c Slater b Fleming	18
S Warne c and b Sohail	14	Wasim Akram not out	45
J Angel b Akram	7	Mushtaq Ahmed c Warne b McDermott	0
C McDermott not out	9	Waqar Younis lbw b Fleming	13
		Mohsin Kamal run out	2
Sundries	14	Sundries	19
Total 9 (Dec)	521	Total	260

Fall of Wickets: 176, 181, 198, 322, 347, 456, 501, 511, 521
Bowling: Wasim Akram 23.5-3-62-1,
Waqar Younis 32-6-112-2, Mohsin Kamal 26-3-109-3,
Mushtaq Ahmed 36-2-145-1, Aamir Sohail 21-3-67-2
Aamir Malik 5-2-16-0, Salim Malik 1-0-4-0

Fall of Wickets: 28, 90, 119, 152, 155, 189, 189, 198, 253, 260
Bowling: C McDermott 22-8-74-4, D Fleming 22-3-75-4, S Warne 21.4-8-58-1, J Angel 11-2-36-0

AUSTRALIA - SECOND INNINGS

M. Slater b Waqar	1
M. Taylor not out	5
D. Boon not out	7

Sundries	1
Total 1 for 14	

Fall of Wickets: 2

Bowling: Waqar Younis 5-3-2-1, Rashid Latif 2-0-10-0, Saeed Anwar 2-2-0-0-, Mushtaq Ahmed 1-0-1-0.

MATCH DRAWN

PAKISTAN SECOND INNINGS

Saeed Anwar c Healy b M Waugh	75
Aamir Sohail c Healy b McDermott	72
Zahid Fazal c Healy b M Waugh	1
Salim Malik c Healy b Fleming	237
Aamir Malik c Bevan b Fleming	65
Inzamam Ul Haq lbw b Fleming	0
Rashid Latif c Bevan b Taylor	38
Wasim Akram c Healy b Angel	5
Mushtaq Ahmed c S Waugh b McDermott	0
Waqar Younis lbw b Slater	10
Mohsin Kamal not out	0

Sundries	34
Total 537	

Fall of Wickets: 79, 227, 336, 469, 469, 478, 495, 496, 537, 537

Bowling: C McDermott 33-3-86-2, D Fleming 26-2-86-3 (includes hat-trick), J Angel 28-1-124-1, M Waugh 16-1-63-2, S Warne 25-6-56-0, M Bevan 4-0-27-0, S Waugh 13-2-41-0, M Slater 1.1-0-4-1, D Boon 3-1-9-0, M Taylor 3-1-11-1

LIMITED OVERS SERIES at Gaddafi Stadium, Lahore, Pakistan
12 October 1994

AUSTRALIA

M Taylor st Richardson b Shaw	56
M Slater st Richardson b Shaw	44
M Waugh c and b Cronje	3
D Boon run out	8
S Waugh c Kirsten b Matthews	56
M Bevan run out	15
I Healy not out	18
G Robertson not out	1

Sundries	6
Total 6 for 207	

Fall of Wickets: 98, 107, 107, 128, 160, 202

Bowling: F De Villiers 9-1-38-0, C Matthews 10-1-41-1 B McMillan 3-0-24-0, E Simons 8-0-37-0, T Shaw 10-0-34-2 H. Cronje 10-1-32-1

Overs: 50

AUSTRALIA WON BY 6 RUNS

SOUTH AFRICA

K Wessels c Healy b Fleming	6
G Kirsten c Healy b Fleming	4
H Cronje not out	98
D Cullinan c Slater b S Waugh	12
J Rhodes lbw b S Waugh	42
B McMillan b M Waugh	3
E Simons b McDermott	19
D Richardson b McDermott	4
C Matthews b McDermott	1
T Shaw not out	1

Sundries	11
Total 8 for 201	

Fall of Wickets: 8, 15, 50, 126, 143, 182, 194

Bowling: C McDermott 10-2-32-3, D Fleming 10-3-29-2, S Waugh 10-0-35-2, S Warne 10-0-39-0, G Robertson 7-0-41-0, M Waugh 3-0-14-1

Overs: 50

LIMITED OVERS SERIES at Qasim-a-Bagh Stadium, Multan, Pakistan
14 October 1994

PAKISTAN

Saeed Anwar b Fleming	22
Aamir Sohail b Fleming	5
Inzamam Ul Haq run out	59
Salim Malik c Healy b Warne	32
Ijaz Ahmed c Healy b McDermott	21
Aamir Malik c Healy b McDermott	20
Wasim Akram b Fleming	9
Rashid Latif b Fleming	16
Akram Raza not out	5
Wazar Younis not out	0
Sundries	11
Total 8 for 200	

Fall of Wickets: 9, 32, 113, 132, 164, 166, 189, 199
Bowling: C McDermott 10-1-34-2, D Fleming 10-0-49-4,
S Waugh 10-1-37-0, S Warne 10-1-29-1,
G Robertson 5-0-24-0, M Waugh 5-0-20-0
Overs: 50
AUSTRALIA WON BY 7 WICKETS

AUSTRALIA

M Slater lbw b Akram	0
M Taylor b Raza	46
M Waugh c Latif by Waqar	0
D Boon not out	84
S Waugh not out	59
Sundries	12
Total 3 for 201	

Wall of Wickets: 10, 11, 82
Bowling: Wasim Akram 8-3-26-1, Waqar Younis
9-0-39-1, Akram Raza 10-0-35-1, Mushtaq
Ahmed 9-0-48-0, Aamir Sohail 6-0-26-0,
Salim Malik 4-0-20-0
Overs: 50

LIMITED OVERS SERIES at Iqbal Stadium, Faisalabad, Pakistan
18 October 1994

AUSTRALIA

M Taylor c Richardson b De Villiers	4
M Slater b Eksteen	38
M Waugh c Richardson b Cronje	38
D Boon c Wessels b Pringle	43
S Waugh b Simons	23
M Bevan not out	36
I Healy c De Villiers b Simons	4
S Warne not out	15
Sundries	7
Total 6 for 208	

Fall of Wickets: 6, 69, 95, 143, 160, 167
Bowling: F De Villiers 9-2-41-1, M Pringle 9-1-49-1,
E Simons 10-0-41-2, H Cronje 10-1-31-1,
C Eksteen 8-0-26-1, D Crookes 4-0-17-0
Overs: 50
AUSTRALIA WON BY 22 RUNS

SOUTH AFRICA

K Wessels c Bevan b May	30
A Hudson run out	5
H Cronje c S Waugh b McDermott	64
J Rhodes c Boon b May	11
G Kirsten b McGrath	24
D Richardson lbw b McGrath	10
E Simons st Healy b Warne	11
D Crookes st Healy b Warne	20
M Pringle lbw b Warne	0
C Eksteen not out	0
F De Villiers st Healy b Warne	0
Sundries	11
Total 186	

Fall of Wickets: 7, 64, 86, 124, 138, 156, 176,
176, 185, 186
Bowling: C McDermott 9-2-34-1, G McGrath
10-2-31-2, S Warne 9.2-0-40-4, T May 10-0-34-2,
S Waugh 10-1-40-0
Overs: 48.2

LIMITED OVERS SERIES at Pindi Stadium, Rawalpindi, Pakistan
22 October 1994

AUSTRALIA

M Slater b Aaqib	4
M Taylor c Raza b Aaqib	14
M Waugh not out	121
J Langer c Saeed b Akram	27
S Waugh lbw b Salim	14
M Bevan b Waqar	22
I Healy run out	16
S Warne not out	11
Sundries	21
Total 6 for 250	

Fall of Wickets: 14, 50, 114, 140, 206, 234
Bowling: Wasim Akram 10-0-47-1, Aaqib Javed 10-0-44-2
Wazar Younis 10-0-50-0, Aamir Sohail 5-0-25-0
Akram Raza 10-0-36-0, Salim Malik 5-0-34-1
Overs: 50
PAKISTAN WON BY 9 WICKETS

PAKISTAN

Saeed Anwar not out	104
Aamir Sohail c Bevan b May	45
Inzamam-Ul-Haq not out	91
Sundries	11
Total 1 for 251	

Fall of Wickets: 91
Bowling: C McDermott 8-1-54-0, G McGrath
6-1-37-0, T May 9-0-65-1, S Warne 9-1-47-0,
S Waugh 5-0-26-0, M Waugh 2-0-15-0
Overs: 39

LIMITED OVERS SERIES at Arbab Niaz Stadium, Peshawar, Pakistan
24 October 1994

SOUTH AFRICA

K Wessels c Bevan b McDermott	4
G Kirsten b McGrath	45
H Cronje not out	100
D Cullinan b Warne	36
J Rhodes c Taylor b Angel	3
D Richardson c Slater b M Waugh	25
D Crookes lbw b McGrath	0
E Simons not out	10
Sundries	28
Total 6 for 251	

Fall of Wickets: 7, 92, 157, 167, 207, 207
Bowling: C McDermott 9-0-48-1, J Angel 10-1-37-1,
G McGrath 10-2-22-2, M Waugh 6-0-39-1, T May 5-0-33-0,
S Warne 10-0-51-1
Overs: 50
AUSTRALIA WON BY 3 WICKETS

AUSTRALIA

M Taylor c Richardson b De Villiers	17
M Slater run out	54
M Waugh c Rhodes b Shaw	43
D Boon run out	39
M Bevan c Shaw b De Villiers	45
J Langer not out	33
S Warne run out	13
J Angel b Matthews	0
C McDermott not out	1
Sundries	7
Total 7 for 252	

Fall of Wickets: 38, 107, 119, 186, 223, 239, 251
Bowling: F De Villiers 10-2-49-2, C Matthews,
9.4-1-43-1, E Simons 8-0-46-0, H Cronje,
10-0-46-0, T Shaw 10-0-49-1, D Crookes 2-0-14-0
Overs: 49.4

LIMITED OVERS SERIES at Jinnah Stadium, Gujranwaza, Pakistan
26 October 1994

AUSTRALIA -V- PAKISTAN
Washed out — no play

LIMITED OVERS SERIES FINAL at Gaddafi Stadium, Lahore, Pakistan
30 October 1994

AUSTRALIA

M Taylor c and b Salim	56
M Slater st Latif b Salim	66
M Waugh b Salim	38
D Boon c Salim b Waqar	21
S Waugh b Sohail	1
M Bevan not out	53
P Emery not out	11

Sundries	23
Total	5 for 269

Fall of Wickets: 121, 146, 188, 191, 226
Bowling: Wasim Akram 10-1-63-0, Aaqib Javed 7-0-30-0,
Waqar Younis 8-0-48-1, Akram Raza 10-0-45-0,
Aamir Sohail 5-0-35-1, Salim Malik 10-0-31-3
Overs: 50
AUSTRALIA WON BY 64 RUNS

PAKISTAN

Saeed Anwar c Taylor b Fleming	0
Aamir Sohail c S Waugh b Fleming	21
Inzamam-Ul-Haq c Emery b McGrath	10
Salim Malik b Fleming	35
Ijaz Ahmed c Emery b McGrath	4
Basit Ali lbw b McGrath	63
Wasim Akram b McGrath	26
Akram Raza c Emery b M Waugh	0
Rashid Latif not out	10
Waqar Younis b McGrath	2
Aaqib Javed b M Waugh	17

Sundries	17
Total	205

Fall of Wickets: 17, 29, 43, 64, 112, 173, 174,
176, 178, 205
Bowling: C McDermott 9-0-32-0, D Fleming
8-2-32-3, G McGrath 10-0-52-5, S Waugh 2-0-6-0,
S Warne 10-2-32-0, M Waugh 7.5-0-43-2
Overs: 46.5

THIRD TEST at Gaddafi Stadium, Lahore, Pakistan
1, 2, 3, 4, 5 November 1994

PAKISTAN — FIRST INNINGS

Saeed Anwar b Warne	30
Aamir Sohail c Emery b McGrath	1
Inzamam-Ul-Haq lbw b May	66
Salim Malik c Bevan b May	75
Ijaz Ahmed c Boon b Warne	48
Basit Ali c M Waugh b Warne	0
Moin Khan not out	115
Akram Raza b Warne	0
Mushtaq Ahmed b May	14
Aaqib Javed c M Waugh b Warne	2
Mohsin Kamal lbw b Warne	4
Sundries	18
Total	373

Fall of Wickets: 8, 34, 157, 204, 209, 294, 294, 346, 355, 373
Bowling: C McDermott 24-4-87-0, G McGrath 24-6-65-1,
S Warne 41.5-12-136-6, T May 29-7-69-3, M Waugh 2-0-4-0

AUSTRALIA — FIRST INNINGS

M Slater c Moin b Kamal	74
M Taylor c Saeed b Mushtaq	32
D Boon c Moin b Raza	5
P Emery not out	8
M Waugh c Moin b Kamal	71
M Bevan c sub (Nadeem) b Mushtaq	91
J Langer c Ijaz b Kamal	69
S Warne c and b Kamal	33
C McDermott c and b Mushtaq	29
T May c Moin b Raza	10
G McGrath b Mushtaq	3
Sundries	30
Total	455

Fall of Wickets: 97, 106, 126, 248, 318, 402, 406, 443, 450, 455
Bowling: Aaqib Javed 31-9-75-0, Mohsin Kamal 28-3-116-4, Mushtaq Ahmed 45.1-6-121-4, Akram Raza 45-9-123-2

PAKISTAN — SECOND INNINGS

Basit Ali c Emery b McGrath	2
Saeed Anwar c Emery b McGrath	32
Inzamam-Ul-Haq c Emery b McDermott	3
Salim Malik b Bevan	143
Ijaz Ahmed lbw b McGrath	6
Moin Khan c McDermott b May	16
Aamir Sohail st Emery b Warne	105
Akram Raza lbw b Warne	32
Mushtaq Ahmed c Emery b McGrath	27
Aaqib Javed b Warne	2
Mohsin Kamal not out	0
Sundries	36
Total	404

Fall of Wickets: 20, 28, 60, 74, 107, 303, 363, 384, 394, 404
Bowling: C McDermott 19-2-81-1, G McGrath 25.1-1-92-4,
S Warne 30-2-104-3. T May 25-4-60-1, M Bevan 4-0-21-1,
M Waugh 6-0-22-0
MATCH DRAWN

Australia -v- Pakistan Tests

AUSTRALIAN TEST BATTING AVERAGES

	M	Inn	N.O.	Runs	H.S.	Avrge	Ct	St
Justin Langer	1	1	-	69	69	69.00	-	-
Michael Bevan	3	4	-	243	91	60.75	5	-
Steve Waugh	2	3	-	171	98	57.00	2	-
Mark Waugh	3	4	-	220	71	55.00	3	-
David Boon	3	5	2	149	114*	49.67	3	-
Michael Slater	3	5	-	244	110	48.80	1	-
Ian Healy	2	3	-	123	58	41.00	8	-
Craig McDermott	2	2	1	38	29	38.00	1	-
Mark Taylor	3	5	1	106	69	26.50	3	-
Shane Warne	3	4	-	69	33	17.25	2	-
Jo Angel	2	3	-	20	8	6.66	1	-
Tim May	2	3	1	12	10	6.00	-	-
Glenn McGrath	2	3	-	4	3	1.33	-	-
Phil Emery	1	1	1	8	8*	-	5	1
Damien Fleming			-	-	-	-	-	-

AUSTRALIAN TEST BOWLING AVERAGES

	M	Overs	Mdns	Runs	Wkts	Avrge	Best
Michael Slater	3	1.1	0	4	1	4.00	1/4
Mark Taylor	3	3.0	1	11	1	11.00	1/11
Damien Fleming	1	48.0	5	161	7	23.00	4/75
Shane Warne	3	181.4	50	504	18	28.00	6/136
Glenn McGrath	2	80.1	15	245	7	35.00	4/92
Tim May	2	92.0	20	251	6	41.83	3/69
Mark Waugh	3	27.0	2	93	2	46.50	2/63
Craig McDermott	2	98.0	17	328	7	46.86	4/74
Michael Bevan	3	8.0	0	48	1	48.00	1/21
Jo Angel	2	80.1	11	306	6	51.00	3/54
Steve Waugh	2	30.0	5	78	1	78.00	1/28
David Boon	3	3.0	1	9	0	-	-

PAKISTAN TEST BATTING AVERAGES

	M	Inn	N.O.	Runs	H.S.	Avrge	Ct	St
Moin Khan	1	2	1	131	115*	131.00	4	-
Salim Malik	3	6	-	557	237	92.83	-	-
Aamir Sohail	3	6	-	328	105	54.66	3	-
Saeed Anwar	3	6	-	314	85	52.33	1	-
Aamir Malik	1	2	-	76	65	38.00	-	-
Wasim Akram	2	4	1	93	45*	31.00	1	-
Inzamam-Ul-Haq	3	6	1	150	66	30.00	1	-
Ijaz Ahmed	1	2	-	54	48	27.00	1	-
Rashid Latif	2	4	-	93	38	23.25	5	-
Mushtaq Ahmed	3	6	2	63	27	15.75	-	-
Akram Raza	3	4	-	47	32	11.75	-	-
Zahid Fazal	2	4	-	41	27	10.25	1	-
Waqar Younis	2	4	-	36	13	9.00	-	-
Basit Ali	2	4	-	14	12	3.50	-	-
Mohsin Kamal	2	4	2	6	4	3.00	2	-
Aaqib Javed	1	2	-	4	2	2.00	-	-

PAKISTAN TEST BOWLING AVERAGES

	M	Overs	Mdns	Runs	Wkts	Avrge	Best
Wasim Akram	2	70.5	10	200	9	22.22	5/64
Waqar Younis	2	74.2	12	258	10	25.80	4/69
Mohsin Kamal	2	54.0	5	225	7	32.14	4/116
Aamir Sohail	3	33.0	3	105	3	35.00	2/67
Mushtaq Ahmed	3	127.1	13	415	9	46.11	4/121
Akram Raza	2	69.0	11	192	2	96.00	2/123
Salim Malik	3	2.0	0	11	0	-	-
Aamir Malik	1	5.0	2	16	0	-	-
Aaqib Javed	1	31.0	9	75	0	-	-
Rashid Latif	2	2.0	0	10	0	-	-
Saeed Anwar	3	2.0	2	0	0	-	-

In Australia, 1994-95

AUSTRALIA — FIRST INNINGS

M Slater c Gatting b Gooch	176
M Taylor run out	59
D Boon b Gough	3
M Waugh c Stewart b Gough	140
M Bevan c Hick b Gough	7
S Warne c Rhodes b Gough	2
S Waugh c Hick b DeFreitas	19
I Healy c Hick b DeFreitas	7
C McDermott c Gough b McCague	2
T May not out	3
G McGrath c Gough b McCague	0
Sundries	8
Total	**426**

Fall of Wickets: 99, 126, 308, 326, 352, 379, 407, 419, 425, 426

Bowling: P DeFreitas 31-8-102-2, M McCague 19.2-4-96-2, D Gough 32-7-107-4, G Hick 4-0-22-0, G Gooch 9-2-20-1

ENGLAND — FIRST INNINGS

M Atherton c Healy b McDermott	54
A Stewart c Healy b McDermott	16
C Hick c Healy b McDermott	3
G Thorpe c and b Warne	28
G Gooch c Healy b May	20
M Gatting lbw b McDermott	10
M McCague b McDermott	1
S Rhodes lbw b McDermott	4
P DeFreitas c Healy b Warne	7
D Gough not out	17
P Tufnell c Taylor b Warne	0
Sundries	7
Total	**167**

Fall of Wickets: 22, 35, 82, 105, 131, 133, 140, 147, 151, 167

Bowling: C McDermott 19-3-53-6, G McGrath 10-2-40-0, T May 17-3-34-1, S Warne 21.2-7-39-3

AUSTRALIA — SECOND INNINGS

M Slater lbw b Gough	45
M Taylor c Stewart b Tufnell	58
D Boon b Tufnell	20
M Waugh b Tufnell	15
M. Bevan c Rhodes b DeFreitas	21
S. Warne c (sub) White b DeFreitas	0
S. Waugh c (sub) White b Tufnell	7
I Healy not out	45
C McDermott c Rhodes b Gough	6
T May not out	9
Sundries	14
Total 8 (dec)	**248**

Fall of Wickets: 109, 117, 139, 174, 183, 190, 191, 201

Bowling: P DeFreitas 22-1-74-2, D Gough 23-3-78-2 P Tufnell 38-10-79-4, G Gooch 3-2-5-0, G Hick 2-1-1-0

AUSTRALIA WON BY 184 RUNS

ENGLAND — SECOND INNINGS

M Atherton lbw b Warne	23
A Stewart b Warne	33
G Hick c Healy b Warne	80
G Thorpe b Warne	67
G Gooch c Healy b Warne	56
M Gatting c Healy b McDermott	13
M McCague lbw b Warne	0
S Rhodes c Healy b McDermott	2
P DeFreitas b Warne	11
D Gough c M Waugh b Warne	10
P Tufnell not out	2
Sundries	26
Total	**323**

Fall of Wickets: 50, 59, 219, 220, 250, 280, 309, 310, 310, 323

Bowling: C McDermott 23-4-90-2, G McGrath 19-4-61-0, S Warne 50.2-22-71-8, T May 35-16-59-0, M Waugh 7-1-17-0, M Bevan 3-0-11-0

WORLD SERIES at WACA, Perth
2 December 1994

ZIMBABWE

A Flower c Warne b Fleming	29
G Flower b McGrath	20
A Campbell hit wicket b Warne	22
D Houghton run out	13
M Dekker lbw b McGrath	16
W James run out	8
G Martin b Law	16
P Strang not out	17
E Brandes c Healy b McDermott	5
H Streak c Fleming b Warne	7
D Brain not out	1
Sundries	12

Total 9 for 166

Fall of Wickets: 49, 56, 83, 88, 109, 117, 144, 151, 164
Bowling: C McDermott 10-0-32-1, D Fleming 10-0-45-1,
G McGrath 10-1-23-2, M Waugh 1-0-3-0,
S Law 9-0-27-1, S Warne 10-1-27-2
Overs: 50
AUSTRALIA WON BY 2 WICKETS

AUSTRALIA

M Slater c A Flower b Streak	18
M Taylor c G Flower b Brandes	45
D Boon c Houghton b Strang	8
M Bevan c James b Streak	30
S Law c Houghton b Martin	7
I Healy c Campbell b G Flower	40
S Warne c and b G Flower	5
C McDermott c Dekker b G Flower	0
M Waugh not out	6
D Fleming not out	0
Sundries	8

Total 8 for 167

Fall of Wickets: 69, 69, 87, 96, 156, 161, 161, 164
Bowling: D Brain 8.2-2-39-0, H Streak 10-1-31-2
E Brandes 10-1-29-1, P Strang 10-1-30-1,
G Martin 5-0-17-1, G Flower 4-0-15-3
Overs: 47.2

WORLD SERIES at SCG, Sydney
6 December 1994

AUSTRALIA

M Taylor c and b Hick	57
M Slater c Hick b Udal	50
M Waugh b Udal	4
D Boon not out	64
M Bevan c Gooch b Gough	46
S Law not out	0
Sundries	3

Total 4 for 224

Fall of Wickets: 96, 106, 126, 218
Bowling: J Benjamin 6-0-25-0, P DeFreitas 9-1-43-0,
D Gough 10-0-51-1, C White 5-0-22-0,
S Udal 10-1-37-2, G Hick 10-0-44-1
Overs: 50
AUSTRALIA WON BY 28 RUNS

ENGLAND

M Atherton lbw b Law	60
A Stewart c Law b May	48
G Hick c Boon b May	6
G Thorpe c Bevan b McDermott	21
G Gooch c McDermott b Warne	21
C White b McDermott	0
S Rhodes c Warne b Law	8
P DeFreitas run out	6
D Gough not out	8
S Udal b McGrath	4
J Benjamin b McDermott	0
Sundries	14

Total 196

Fall of Wickets: 100, 112, 133, 147, 149, 164, 180, 187, 195, 196
Bowling: C McDermott 9.3-0-34-3, G McGrath 9-4-22-1,
S Warne 10-0-46-1, S Law 10-0-52-2, T May 10-1-35-2
Overs: 48.3

WORLD SERIES *at Bellerive, Hobart*
8 December 1994

AUSTRALIA

M Slater c Whittall b Brain	10
S Law c G Flower b Dekker	110
M Waugh c G Flower b Whittall	12
D Boon not out	98
M Bevan not out	11

Sundries 13

Total 3 for 254

Fall of Wickets: 12, 55, 214

Bowling: D Brain 10-1-51-1, H Streak 9-0-55-0, G Whittall 7-1-22-1, M Dekker 10-0-42-1, P Strang 9-0-51-0, G Flower 5-0-26-0

Overs: 50

AUSTRALIA WON BY 84 RUNS

ZIMBABWE

A Flower c Healy b May	39
G Flower c Healy b McGrath	8
A Campbell b McGrath	1
D Houghton b May	4
M Dekker run out	11
G Whittall c Healy b Fleming	35
W James c Healy b Warne	15
I Butchart b Fleming	10
P Strang not out	21
H Streak not out	12

Sundries 14

Total 8 for 170

Fall of Wickets: 15, 24, 47, 64, 73, 117, 129, 136

Bowling: G McGrath 8-2-18-2, D Fleming 10-0-42-2, T May 10-1-34-2, S Law 10-1-25-0, S Warne 9-0-23-1, D Boon 2-0-11-0, M Slater 1-0-11-0

Overs: 50

WORLD SERIES *at Adelaide Oval, Adelaide*
11 December 1994

AUSTRALIA

M Taylor b Robertson	44
M Slater c Hayden b Rowell	64
M Waugh b Hughes	0
D Boon c Langer b Hughes	39
M Bevan c Emery b Robertson	4
S Law b Moody	0
I Healy c Hayden b Reiffel	15
S Warne c Langer b Hughes	8
C McDermott not out	10
T May run out	1
G McGrath c Langer b Reiffel	0

Sundries 17

Total 202

Fall of Wickets: 93, 94, 132, 151, 152, 175, 181, 197, 199, 202

Bowling: G Rowell 10-0-41-1, P Reiffel 9.3-2-34-2, T Moody 7-0-36-1, M Hughes 9-0-33-3, D Martyn 3-0-20-0, G Robertson 10-1-27-2

Overs: 48.3

AUSTRALIA A

D Lehmann c Healy b McGrath	4
M Hayden c Taylor b Law	45
D Martyn b Warne	37
J Langer c Law b Warne	1
R Ponting c Bevan b Warne	42
T Moody c (sub) Fleming b May	5
P Emery run out	30
G Robertson not out	19
P Reiffel lbw b McGrath	0
G Rowell c Law b McGrath	0
M Hughes c Law b McGrath	1

Sundries 12

Total 196

Fall of Wickets: 10, 71, 77, 108, 117, 157, 190, 190, 190, 196

Bowling: C McDermott 9-0-33-0, G McGrath 9.3-0-43-4, M Waugh 4-1-17-0, S Warne 10-1-40-3, T May 10-0-29-1, S Law 5-0-28-1

Overs: 47.3

AUSTRALIA WON BY 6 RUNS

THE STORY IN STATS

SECOND TEST at the MCG, Melbourne
24, 26, 27, 28, 29 December 1994

AUSTRALIA — FIRST INNINGS		ENGLAND — FIRST INNINGS	
M Slater run out	3	M Atherton lbw b Warne	44
M Taylor lbw b DeFreitas	9	A Stewart c and b Warne	16
D Boon c Hick b Tufnell	41	G Hick c Healy b McDermott	23
M Waugh c Thorpe b DeFreitas	71	G Thorpe c M Waugh b Warne	51
M. Bevan c Atherton b Gough	3	G Gooch c and b McDermott	15
S. Waugh not out	94	M Gatting c S Waugh b Warne	9
I Healy c Rhodes b Tufnell	17	D Gough c Healy b McDermott	20
S Warne c Hick b Gough	6	S Rhodes c M Waugh b Warne	0
T May lbw b Gough	9	P DeFreitas st Healy b Warne	14
C McDermott b Gough	0	D Malcolm not out	11
D Fleming c Hick b Malcolm	16	P Tufnell run out	0
Sundries	10	Sundries	9
Total	**279**	**Total**	**212**

Fall of Wickets: 10, 39, 91, 100, 171, 208, 220, 242, 242, 279

Fall of Wickets: 40, 119, 124, 140, 148, 151, 185, 189, 207, 212

Bowling: D Malcolm 28.3-4-78-1, P DeFreitas 23-4-66-2, D Gough 26-9-60-4, P Tufnell 28-7-59-2, G Hick 2-0-9-0

Bowling: C McDermott 24-6-72-3, D Fleming 11-5-30-0, M Waugh 3-0-11-0, S Warne 27.4-8-64-6, T May 18-5-28-0

AUSTRALIA — SECOND INNINGS		ENGLAND — SECOND INNINGS	
M Slater st Rhodes b Tufnell	44	G Gooch c Healy b Fleming	2
M Taylor lbw b Gough	19	M Atherton c Healy b McDermott	25
D Boon lbw b DeFreitas	131	G Hick B Fleming	2
M Waugh c and b Gough	29	G Thorpe c Healy b McDermott	9
M Bevan c (sub) Crawley b Tufnell	17	M Gatting c Taylor b McDermott	25
S Waugh not out	26	S Rhodes c M Waugh b McDermott	16
I Healy c Thorpe b Tufnell	17	A Stewart not out	8
S Warne c DeFreitas b Gough	0	P DeFreitas lbw b Warne	0
C McDermott not out	2	D Gough c Healy b Warne	0
		D Malcolm c Boon b Warne	0
		P Tufnell c Healy b McDermott	0
Sundries	17	Sundries	5
Total	**7 (dec) 320**	**Total**	**92**

Fall of Wickets: 61, 81, 157, 269, 275, 316, 317

Fall of Wickets: 3, 10, 23, 43, 81, 88, 91, 91, 91, 92

Bowling: D Malcolm 22-3-86-0, P DeFreitas 26-2-70-1, P Tufnell 48-8-90-3, D Gough 25-6-59-3, G Hick 3-2-5-0

Bowling: C McDermott 16.5-5-42-5, D Fleming 9-1-24-2, S Warne 13-6-16-3 (includes hat-trick), T May 4-1-8-0

AUSTRALIA WON BY 295 RUNS

THIRD TEST at the SCG Sydney
1, 2, 3, 4, 5 January 1995

ENGLAND — FIRST INNINGS

G Gooch c Healy b Fleming	1
M Atherton b McDermott	88
G Hick b McDermott	2
G Thorpe lbw b McDermott	10
J Crawley c M Waugh b Fleming	72
M Gatting c Healy b McDermott	0
A Fraser c Healy b Fleming	27
S Rhodes run out	1
D Gough c Fleming b McDermott	51
D Malcolm b Warne	29
P Tufnell not out	4
Sundries	24
Total	309

Fall of Wickets: 1, 10, 20, 194, 194, 196, 197, 255, 295
Bowling: C McDermott 30-7-101-5, P Tufnell 28-7-59-2,
G Hick 2-0-9-0, S Warne 36-10-88-1, T May 17-4-35-0,
M Waugh 6-1-10-0, M Bevan 4-1-8-0,
D Fleming 26-2-12-52-3

AUSTRALIA — FIRST INNINGS

M Slater b Malcolm	11
M Taylor c and b Gough	49
D Boon b Gough	3
M Waugh c Rhodes b Malcolm	3
M Bevan c Thorpe b Fraser	8
S Waugh b Gough	1
I Healy c Hick b Gough	10
S Warne c Gatting b Fraser	0
T May c Hick b Gough	0
C McDermott not out	21
D Fleming b Gough	0
Sundries	10
Total	116

Fall of Wickets: 12, 15, 18, 38, 39, 57, 62, 65, 116, 116
Bowling: D Malcolm 13-4-34-2, D Gough 18.5-4-49-6,
A Fraser 11-1-26-2

ENGLAND — SECOND INNINGS

G Gooch lbw b Fleming	29
M Atherton c Taylor b Fleming	67
G Hick not out	98
G Thorpe not out	47
Sundries	14
Total 2 (dec)	255

Fall of Wickets: 54, 158
Bowling: C McDermott 24-2-76-0, D Fleming 20-3-66-2
M Waugh 2-1-4-0, S Warne 16-2-48-0, T May 10-1-55-0
MATCH DRAWN

AUSTRALIA — SECOND INNINGS

M Slater c Tufnell b Fraser	103
M Taylor b Malcolm	113
D Boon c Hick b Gough	17
M Waugh lbw b Fraser	25
M Bevan c Rhodes b Fraser	7
S Waugh c Rhodes b Fraser	0
I Healy c Rhodes b Fraser	5
S Warne not out	36
T May not out	10
Sundries	28
Total 7 for	344

Fall of Wickets: 208, 239, 265, 282, 286, 289, 292
Bowling: D Malcolm 21-4-75, D Gough 28-4-72-1,
A Fraser 25-3-73-5, P Tufnell 35.4-9-61-0,
G Hick 5-0-21-0, G Gooch 7-1-27-0

WORLD SERIES at the GABBA, Brisbane
8 January 1995

AUSTRALIA

M Taylor c Reiffel b Blewett	17
M Slater c Bevan b Reiffel	9
M Waugh c Blewett b Hughes	93
D Boon not out	86
S Waugh c Hughes b George	23
S Law c Hayden b Reiffel	12
C McDermott not out	5

Sundries	7
Total 5 for 252	

Fall of Wickets: 17, 65, 163, 213, 241
Bowling: M Hughes 10-0-55-1, P Reiffel 10-0-46-2,
S George 10-0-54-1, G Blewett 10-0-46-1,
G Robertson 10-0-47-0
Overs: 50
AUSTRALIA WON BY 34 RUNS

AUSTRALIA A

M Hayden b Law	51
G Blewett c M Waugh b Law	63
R Ponting run out	39
M Bevan run out	14
J Langer b McDermott	1
D Martyn c M Waugh b McGrath	12
M Hughes b Fleming	3
P Reiffel c S Waugh b Fleming	4
G Robertson not out	6
M Atkinson b Law	11
S George b McDermott	4

Sundries	10
Total 218	

Fall of Wickets: 104, 131, 166, 172, 176, 180, 190, 196,
213, 218
Bowling: C McDermott 8.5-1-29-2, D Fleming 10-1-35-2,
G McGrath 10-0-62-1, T May 6-0-20-0, S Law 9-0-46-3,
D Boon 4-0-17-0
Overs: 47.5

WORLD SERIES at the MCG, Melbourne
10 January 1995

ENGLAND

G Gooch c Taylor b McGrath	2
M Atherton c S Waugh b M Waugh	14
G Hick c Fleming b Warne	91
G Thorpe c Healy b M Waugh	8
N Fairbrother c Healy b Warne	35
J Crawley c Healy b McGrath	2
S Rhodes lbw b McGrath	2
D Gough b McGrath	45
P DeFreitas not out	2
S Udal not out	2

Sundries	22
Total 8 for 225	

Fall of Wickets: 11, 31, 44, 133, 136, 142, 216, 223
Bowling: D Fleming 10-1-36-0, G McGrath 10-1-25-4,
M Waugh 10-1-43-2, S Warne 10-0-37-2,
G Robertson 5-0-38-0, S Law 5-0-32-0
Overs: 50
ENGLAND WON BY 37 RUNS

AUSTRALIA

M Taylor c Rhodes b Fraser	6
M Slater b Fraser	2
M Waugh b Hick	41
S Waugh c Rhodes b Fraser	0
S Law c and b Udal	17
D Boon b Hick	26
I Healy c Atherton b Hick	56
G Robertson run out	1
S Warne b Fraser	21
D Fleming not out	5
G McGrath b DeFreitas	10

Sundries	3
Total 188	

Fall of Wickets: 3, 16, 19, 62, 76, 125, 131, 173, 179, 188
Bowling: A Fraser 10-2-22-4, P DeFreitas 9-0-32-1,
G Gooch 10-0-50-0, S Udal 9-1-43-1, G Hick 10-1-41-3
Overs: 48

WORLD SERIES at the SCG Sydney, First Final
15 January 1995

AUSTRALIA A

G Blewett b McDermott	19
M Hayden c Slater b M Waugh	50
D Martyn c Taylor b Warne	20
M Bevan b McDermott	73
J Langer b McDermott	7
R Ponting b McGrath	19
P Emery run out	4
G Robertson c Taylor b McDermott	5
G Rowell not out	1
P McIntyre not out	1
Sundries	10
Total 8 for	209

Fall of Wickets: 28, 69, 105, 136, 192, 196, 203, 203
Bowling: C McDermott 10-0-25-4, D Fleming 10-2-38-0,
C McGrath 10-1-44-1, S Warne 10-2-37-1,
M Waugh 5-0-30-1, S Law 5-0-27-0
Overs: 50
AUSTRALIA WON BY 5 WICKETS

AUSTRALIA

M Slater b Blewett	92
M Taylor b George	16
M Waugh c Bevan b Blewett	16
D Boon c Ponting b McIntyre	36
S Waugh not out	21
S Law st Emery b McIntyre	13
I Healy not out	9
Sundries	10
Total 5 for	213

Fall of Wickets: 51, 80, 167, 167, 190
Bowling: G Rowell 10-1-52-0, S George 9-0-42-1,
G Blewett 10-2-25-2, G Robertson 10-0-35-0,
P McIntyre 10-0-48-2, D Martyn 1-0-7-0
Overs: 50

WORLD SERIES at the MCG Melbourne, Second Final
17 January 1995

AUSTRALIA A

G Blewett c Taylor b McGrath	64
M Hayden c Slater b Fleming	4
D Martyn lbw b Warne	58
M Bevan c Healy b McGrath	19
J Langer c Healy b McGrath	14
R Ponting c M Waugh b Fleming	13
P Emery b Boon	10
G Robertson b Fleming	4
J Angel not out	15
G Rowell c Slater b McDermott	8
S George b Fleming	2
Sundries	15
Total	226

Fall of Wickets: 12, 111, 144, 158, 174, 191, 193, 197
218, 226
Bowling: C McDermott 10-1-38-1, D Fleming 9.4-1-28-4,
G McGrath 10-0-41-3, S Warne 10-0-55-1,
S Law 2-0-21-0, M Waugh 3-0-20-0, D Boon 5-0-13-1
Overs: 49.4
AUSTRALIA WON BY 6 WICKETS
AUSTRALIA WON FINAL SERIES 2-0

AUSTRALIA

M Taylor c Langer b Blewett	50
M Slater run out	56
M Waugh lbw b Blewett	3
D Boon c Martyn b Angel	27
S Waugh not out	56
S Law not out	27
Sundries	10
Total 4 for	229

Fall of Wickets: 107, 111, 116, 172
Bowling: J Angel 10-0-55-1, G Rowell 10-1-40-0,
S George 8-0-34-0, G Blewett 10-1-44-2,
G Robertson 10-0-40-0, D Martyn 1-0-8-0
Overs: 49

FOURTH TEST at the Adelaide Oval, Adelaide
26, 27, 28, 29, 30 January 1995

ENGLAND — FIRST INNINGS

G Gooch c M Waugh b Fleming	47
M Atherton c Boon b Fleming	80
M Gatting c S Waugh b McIntyre	117
G Thorpe c Taylor b Warne	26
J Crawley b Warne	28
S Rhodes c Taylor b McDermott	6
C Lewis c Blewett b McDermott	10
P DeFreitas c Blewett b McIntyre	21
A Fraser run out	7
D Malcolm b McDermott	0
P Tufnell not out	0
Sundries	11
Total	353

Fall of Wickets: 93, 175, 211, 286, 293, 307, 334, 353, 353, 353

Bowling: C McDermott 41-15-66-3, D Fleming 25-6-65-2, G Blewett 16-4-59-0, S Warne 31-9-72-2, P McIntyre 19.3-3-51-2, M Waugh 9-1-33-0

AUSTRALIA — FIRST INNINGS

M Slater c Atherton b DeFreitas	67
M Taylor lbw b Lewis	90
D Boon c Rhodes b DeFreitas	0
M Waugh c Rhodes b Fraser	39
S Waugh c Atherton b Lewis	19
G Blewett not out	102
I Healy c Rhodes b Malcolm	74
S Warne c Thorpe b Fraser	7
D Fleming c Rhodes b Malcolm	0
P McIntyre b Malcolm	0
C McDermott c Frawley b Fraser	5
Sundries	16
Total	419

Fall of Wickets: 128, 130, 202, 207, 232, 396, 405, 406, 414, 419

Bowling: D Malcolm 26-5-78-3, A Fraser 28.5-6-95-3, P Tufnell 24-5-64-0, P DeFreitas 20-3-70-2, C Lewis 18-1-81-2, G Gooch 5-0-22-0

ENGLAND — SECOND INNINGS

G Gooch c Healy b McDermott	34
M Atherton lbw b M Waugh	14
M Gatting b M Waugh	0
G Thorpe c Warne b McDermott	83
J Crawley c and b M Waugh	71
S Rhodes c Fleming b Warne	2
C Lewis b Fleming	7
P DeFreitas c Healy b M Waugh	88
A Fraser c McDermott b M Waugh	5
D Malcolm not out	0
P Tufnell lbw b Warne	0
Sundries	14
Total	328

Fall of Wickets: 26, 30, 83, 154, 169, 181, 270, 317, 317, 328

Bowling: C McDermott 27-5-96-2, D Fleming 11-3-37-1, S Warne 30.5-9-82-2, M Waugh 14-4-40-5, P McIntyre 8-0-36-0, C Blewett 4-0-23-0

ENGLAND WON BY 106 RUNS

AUSTRALIA — SECOND INNINGS

M Slater c Tufnell b Malcolm	5
M Taylor c Thorpe b Malcolm	13
D Boon c Rhodes b Fraser	4
M Waugh c Gatting b Tufnell	24
S Waugh b Malcolm	0
G Blewett c Rhodes b Lewis	12
I Healy not out	51
S Warne lbw b Lewis	2
D Fleming lbw b Lewis	24
P McIntyre lbw b Malcolm	0
C McDermott c Rhodes b Lewis	0
Sundries	21
Total	156

Fall of Wickets: 17, 22, 22, 23, 64, 75, 83, 83, 152, 156

Bowling: D Malcolm 16.1-3-39-4, A Fraser 12-1-37-1, P DeFreitas 11-3-31-0, C Lewis 13-4-24-4, P Tufnell 9-3-17-1

FIFTH TEST at the WACA, Perth
3, 4, 5, 6, 7 February 1995

AUSTRALIA — FIRST INNINGS

M Slater c Lewis b DeFreitas	124
M Taylor c Rhodes b Lewis	9
D Boon c Ramprakash b Lewis	1
M Waugh c DeFreitas b Lewis	88
S Waugh not out	99
G Blewett c Rhodes b Fraser	20
I Healy c Lewis b DeFreitas	12
S Warne c Rhodes b DeFreitas	1
J Angel run out	11
G McGrath run out	0
C McDermott run out	6

Sundries	31
Total	402

Fall of Wickets: 47, 55, 238, 247, 287, 320, 328, 386, 388, 402

Bowling: D Malcolm 31-6-93-0, P DeFreitas 29-8-91-3, A Fraser 32-11-84-1, C Lewis 31.5-8-73-3, G Gooch 1-1-0-0, M Ramprakash 11-0-43-0

ENGLAND — FIRST INNINGS

G Gooch lbw b M Waugh	37
M Atherton c Healy b McGrath	4
M Gatting b McGrath	0
G Thorpe st Healy b Warne	123
J Crawley c Warne b M Waugh	0
M Ramprakash b Warne	72
S Rhodes b Angel	2
C Lewis c Blewett b McGrath	40
P DeFreitas b Angel	0
A Fraser c Warne b Angel	9
D Malcolm not out	0

Sundries	8
Total	295

Fall of Wickets: 5, 5, 77, 77, 235, 246, 246, 247, 293, 295

Bowling: J Angel 22.3-7-65-3, G McGrath 25-6-88-3, G Blewett 4-1-9-0, M Waugh 9-2-29-2, S Warne 23-8-58-2, C McDermott 13-5-41-0

AUSTRALIA — SECOND INNINGS

M Slater c Atherton b Fraser	45
M Taylor b Fraser	52
J Angel run out	0
D Boon c Rhodes b Malcolm	18
M Waugh c Rhodes b DeFreitas	1
S Waugh c Ramprakash b Lewis	80
G Blewett c Malcolm b Lewis	115
I Healy not out	11
S Warne c Lewis b Malcolm	6

Sundries	17
Total 8 (dec)	345

Fall of Wickets: 75, 79, 102, 115, 123, 326, 333, 345

Bowling: D Malcolm 23.3-3-105-2, A Fraser 21-3-74-2, C Lewis 16-1-71-2, P DeFreitas 22-10-54-1, M Ramprakash 8-1-31-0

AUSTRALIA WON BY 329 RUNS

ENGLAND — SECOND INNINGS

G Gooch c and b McDermott	4
M Atherton c Healy b McGrath	8
M Gatting b McDermott	8
A Fraser lbw b McGrath	5
G Thorpe c Taylor b McGrath	0
J Crawley c M Waugh b McDermott	0
M Ramprakash c S Waugh b M Waugh	42
C Rhodes not out	39
C Lewis lbw b McDermott	11
P DeFreitas c Taylor b McDermott	0
D Malcolm b McDermott	0

Sundries	6
Total	123

Fall of Wickets: 4, 17, 26, 26, 27, 27, 95, 121, 123, 123

Bowling: C McDermott 15-4-38-6, G McGrath 13-4-40-3, J Angel 3-0-20-0, S Warne 7-3-11-0, M Waugh 3-0-13-1

Australia -v- England Tests

Full Test Averages

AUSTRALIAN TEST BATTING AVERAGES

	M	Inn	N.O	Runs	H.S	Avrge	Ct	ST
Greg Blewett	2	4	1	249	115	83.00	3	-
Michael Slater	5	10	-	623	176	62.30	-	-
Steve Waugh	5	10	3	345	99*	49.29	3	-
Mark Taylor	5	10	-	471	113	47.10	7	-
Mark Waugh	5	10	-	435	140	43.50	8	-
Ian Healy	5	10	3	249	74	35.57	23	2
David Boon	5	10	-	246	131	24.60	2	-
Tim May	3	5	3	31	10*	15.50	-	-
Michael Bevan	3	6	-	81	35	13.50	-	-
Damien Fleming	3	4	-	40	24	10.00	2	-
Craig McDermott	5	8	2	42	21*	7.00	3	-
Shane Warne	5	10	1	60	36*	6.67	5	-
Jo Angel	1	2	-	11	11	5.50	-	-
Peter McIntyre	1	2	-	0	0	0.00	-	-
Glenn McGrath	2	2	-	0	0	0.00	-	-

AUSTRALIAN TEST BOWLING AVERAGES

	M	Overs	Mdns	Runs	Wkts	Avrge	Best
Mark Waugh	5	53.0	10	157	8	19.63	5/40
Shane Warne	5	256.1	84	549	27	20.33	8/71
Craig McDermott	5	232.5	56	675	32	21.09	6/38
Damien Fleming	3	102.2	30	274	10	27.40	3/52
Jo Angel	1	25.3	7	85	3	28.33	3/65
Glenn McGrath	2	67.0	16	229	6	38.17	3/40
Peter McIntyre	1	27.3	3	87	2	43.50	2/51
Tim May	3	101.0	30	219	1	219.00	1/34
Greg Blewett	2	24.0	5	91	-	-	-
Michael Bevan	3	7.0	1	19	-	-	-

ENGLAND TEST BATTING AVERAGES

	M	Inn	N.O.	Runs	H.S.	Avrge	Ct	St
Mark Ramprakash	1	2	-	114	72	57.00	2	-
Graham Thorpe	5	10	1	444	123	49.33	5	-
Graeme Hick	3	6	1	208	98*	41.60	9	-
Michael Atherton	5	10	-	407	88	40.70	4	-
John Crawley	3	5	-	171	72	34.20	1	-
Graham Gooch	5	10	-	245	56	24.50	-	-
Darren Gough	3	5	1	98	51	24.50	4	-
Alec Stewart	2	4	1	73	33	24.33	2	-
Mike Gatting	5	9	-	182	117	20.22	3	-
Phil DeFreitas	4	8	-	141	88	17.63	2	-
Chris Lewis	2	4	-	68	40	17.00	3	-
Devon Malcolm	4	7	3	50	29	12.50	1	-
Angus Fraser	3	5	-	53	27	10.60	-	-
Steve Rhodes	5	9	1	72	39*	9.00	20	1
Phil Tufnell	4	7	3	6	4*	1.50	2	-
Martin McCague	1	2	-	1	1	0.50	-	-

ENGLAND TEST BOWLING AVERAGES

	M	Overs	Mdns	Runs	Wkts	Avrge	Best
Darren Gough	3	152.5	33	425	20	21.25	6/49
Chris Lewis	2	78.5	14	249	11	22.64	4/24
Angus Fraser	3	129.5	25	389	14	27.79	5/73
Phil DeFreitas	4	184.0	39	558	13	42.92	3/91
Phil Tufnell	4	207.4	45	442	10	44.20	4/79
Devon Malcolm	4	181.1	32	588	13	45.23	4/39
Martin McCague	1	19.2	4	96	2	48.00	2/96
Graham Gooch	5	25.0	6	74	1	74.00	1/20
Graham Hick	3	16.0	3	58	-	-	
Mark Ramprakash	1	19.0	1	74	-	-	

In New Zealand, 1995

LIMITED OVERS CENTENARY TOURNAMENT at Basin Reserve, Wellington
15 February 1995

SOUTH AFRICA

G Kirsten c Healy b Reiffel	15
M Rindel c Taylor b Reiffel	14
H Cronje c Taylor b Blewett	22
D Cullinan st Healy b Warne	0
J Rhodes b McGrath	25
D Callaghan c S Waugh b Warne	1
D Richardson not out	22
E Simons lbw b McGrath	0
P Symcox c M Waugh b May	10
F De Villiers b Reiffel	8
A Donald b Reiffel	0
Sundries	6
Total	123

Fall of Wickets: 20, 48, 52, 54, 55, 95, 95, 111, 121, 123
Bowling: G McGrath 10-1-25-2, P Reiffel 8.2-1-27-4,
G Blewett 10-0-30-1, S Warne 10-3-18-2, T May 8-0-20-1
Overs: 46.2
AUSTRALIA WON BY 3 WICKETS

AUSTRALIA

M Taylor c Cullinan b De Villiers	24
G Blewett run out	14
M Waugh b Symcox	11
D Boon lbw b De Villiers	1
S Waugh not out	44
R Ponting b Simons	1
I Healy lbw b Cronje	18
P Reiffel c Rhodes b Cronje	8
S Warne not out	2
Sundries	1
Total 7 for	124

Fall of Wickets: 38, 38, 39, 55, 56, 103, 115
Bowling: A Donald 7-0-32-0, F De Villiers 10-2-34-2,
E Simons 10-3-19-1, P Symcox 10-1-23-1,
H Cronje 6.2-1-15-2
Overs: 43.2

LIMITED OVERS CENTENARY TOURNAMENT at Eden Park, Auckland
19 February 1995

AUSTRALIA

G Blewett c Fleming b Thomson	3
M Taylor c and b Pringle	97
M Waugh c and b Vaughan	74
D Boon c Larsen b Morrison	44
S Waugh b Pringle	13
P Ponting not out	10
I Healy not out	4
Sundries	9
Total 5 for	254

Fall of Wickets: 3, 150, 214, 238, 241
Bowling: D Morrison 10-1-40-1, S Thomson 10-1-43-1,
C Pringle 10-0-54-2, C Cairns 3-0-21-0, G Larsen 10-0-49-0,
J Vaughan 7-0-41-1
Overs: 50
AUSTRALIA WON BY 27 RUNS

NEW ZEALAND

B Young b Reiffel	4
M Greatbatch c Healy b Reiffel	74
K Rutherford st Healy b Warne	7
S Fleming c Warne b May	53
C Cairns lbw b McGrath	22
S Thomson run out	9
A Parore not out	27
J Vaughan c Healy b Reiffel	3
G Larsen c Reiffel b M Waugh	3
C Pringle b McGrath	4
D Morrison not out	3
Sundries	18
Total 9 for	227

Fall of Wickets: 19, 42, 124, 169, 181, 187, 193, 199, 217
Bowling: G McGrath 10-0-40-2, P Reiffel 10-4-35-3,
S Warne 10-1-40-1, T May 10-0-43-1, G Blewett 2-0-18-0,
D Boon 4-0-20-0, M Waugh 4-0-19-1
Overs: 50

TAYLOR MADE

LIMITED OVERS CENTENARY TOURNAMENT at Carisbrook, Dunedin
22 February 1995

AUSTRALIA

D Boon c Kambli b Vaidya	32
G Blewett c and b Tendulkar	46
R Ponting c Vaidya b Prabhakar	62
S Waugh c and b Kumble	23
M Waugh c Azharuddin b Srinath	48
I Healy not out	21
M Taylor b Srinath	0
S Warne not out	5
Sundries	13
Total 6 for 250	

Fall of Wickets: 56, 103, 158, 207, 226, 226

Bowling: M Prabhakar 10-0-61-1, J Srinath 9-0-49-2,
P Vaidya 7-0-36-1, A Kumble 7-0-28-1, A Kapoor 9-0-38-0
S Tendulkar 8-0-33-1
Overs: 50
INDIA WON BY 5 WICKETS

INDIA

M Prabhakar b Angel	50
S Tendulkar c Taylor b Angel	47
N Sidhu run out	54
M Azharuddin c Healy b Blewett	25
V Kambli not out	51
S Manjrekar c Healy b May	14
N Mongia not out	6
Sundries	5
Total 5 for 252	

Fall of Wickets: 97, 100, 144, 213, 233

Bowling: G McGrath 9-1-45-0, J Angel 10-1-47-2,
S Warne 10-0-61-0, T May 10-0-51-1, G Blewett 8.5-0-47-1
Overs: 47.5

LIMITED OVERS CENTENARY TOURNAMENT FINAL
at Eden Park, Auckland 26 February 1995

NEW ZEALAND

M Greatbatch c McGrath b Reiffel	8
M Douglas c Healy b Reiffel	2
K Rutherford c Boon b May	46
S Fleming c Healy b M Waugh	0
C Cairns c Taylor b May	17
S Thomson c and b Warne	9
A Parore c Taylor b Warne	2
J Vaughan not out	20
G Larsen run out	0
C Pringle b May	1
D Morrison not out	4
Sundries	28
Total 9 for 137	

Fall of Wickets: 8, 29, 35, 81, 102, 106, 106, 106, 112

Bowling: G McGrath 9-1-25-0, P Reiffel 10-3-14-2,
M Waugh 10-1-38-1, S Warne 10-2-21-2, T May 10-2-19-3
G Blewett 1-0-9-0
Overs: 50
AUSTRALIA WON FINAL BY 6 WICKETS

AUSTRALIA

G Blewett c and b Pringle	7
M Taylor St Parore b Vaughan	44
M Waugh c Parore b Morrison	46
D Boon not out	24
S Waugh c Rutherford b Thomson	1
R Ponting not out	7
Sundries	9
Total 4 for 138	

Fall of Wickets: 15, 93, 116, 121

Bowling: D Morrison 9-1-31-1, C Pringle 9.1-1-52-1,
S Thomson 5-0-22-1, J Vaughan 6-1-18-1, G Larsen 2-0-12-0
Overs: 31.1

In The West Indies, 1995

FIRST LIMITED OVERS INTERNATIONAL at Kensington Oval, Bridgetown Barbados
8 March 1995

WEST INDIES

P Simmons c Taylor b Warne	37
S Williams c Healy b Reiffel	11
B Lara c Taylor b Blewett	55
R Richardson run out	9
C Hooper c May b McDermott	84
J Adams c M Waugh b McDermott	2
J Murray c Healy b M Waugh	12
W Benjamin c May b McDermott	22
V Drakes c Warne b M Waugh	9
C Ambrose c Taylor b M Waugh	0
C Walsh not out	6
Sundries	10
Total	257

Fall of Wickets: 26, 69, 87 155, 158, 191, 241, 242, 246, 257
Bowling: C McDermott 10-0-25-3, P Reiffel 10-1-50-1,
M Waugh 6.4-0-42-3, S Warne 10-0-56-1, G Blewett 8-0-44-1
T May 5-0-36-0
Overs: 49.4
WEST INDIES WON BY 6 RUNS

AUSTRALIA

M Taylor c Simmons b Walsh	41
M Slater c Adams b Benjamin	21
M Waugh c Murray b Walsh	29
D Boon not out	85
S Waugh b Drakes	26
G Blewett c Walsh b Ambrose	33
I Healy run out	0
P Reiffel not out	10
Sundries	6
Total 6 for	251

Fall of Wickets: 50, 94, 94, 156, 235, 236
Bowling: C Ambrose 10-1-43-1, C Walsh 10-1-52-2,
W Benjamin 6.1-0-24-1, V Drakes 9.5-0-39-1,
C Hooper 5-0-46-0, P Simmons 9-0-46-0
Overs: 50

SECOND LIMITED OVERS INTERNATIONAL Queens Park Oval, Port of Spain, Trinidad
11 March 1995

AUSTRALIA

M Slater c and b Hooper	55
M Taylor c Walsh b Ambrose	16
M Waugh b Benjamin	0
D Boon c Benjamin b Simmons	48
S Waugh b Walsh	58
G Blewett run out	4
I Healy run out	51
P Reiffel b Benjamin	14
S Warne not out	4
Sundries	10
Total 8 for	260

Fall of Wickets: 37, 39, 93, 153, 162, 207, 252, 260
Bowling: C Ambrose 10-0-47-1, C Walsh 8-0-59-1,
W Benjamin 10-0-49-2, V Drakes 10-0-47-0,
C Hooper 7-0-33-1, P Simmons 5-0-22-1
Overs: 50
AUSTRALIA WON BY 26 RUNS

WEST INDIES

P Simmons b McGrath	34
S Williams lbw b Reiffel	0
B Lara c Healy b Blewett	62
C Hooper c Blewett b Warne	55
J Adams run out	15
K Arthurton c Boon b McDermott	35
J Murray lbw b Reiffel	0
W Benjamin b Reiffel	3
V Drakes c Reiffel b McDermott	16
C Ambrose b McDermott	1
C Walsh not out	0
Sundries	13
Total	234

Fall of Wickets: 5, 79, 121, 175, 182, 185, 191, 232,
234, 234
Bowling: C McDermott 6.5-0-37-3, P Reiffel 10-2-32-3,
G McGrath 9-1-36-1, S Warne 10-0-63-1,
G Blewett 8-0-43-1, S Waugh 4-0-15-0
Overs: 47.5

TAYLOR MADE

THIRD LIMITED OVERS INTERNATIONAL at Queens Park Oval,Port of Spain, Trinidad
12 March 1995

WEST INDIES

P Simmons c Healy b Fleming	6
S Williams run out	6
B Lara c Reiffel b S Waugh	139
C Hooper c Slater b Reiffel	41
J Adams not out	51
K Arthurton c Boon b S Waugh	12
J Murray not out	4

Sundries	23
Total 5 for 282	

Fall of Wickets: 17, 26, 125, 260, 276
Bowling: P Reiffel 10-0-36-1 D Fleming 7.3-1-27-1,
G McGrath 10-0-57-0, S Warne 10-1-52-0,
G Blewett 3-0-32-0, S Waugh 9.3-1-61-2
Overs: 50
WEST INDIES WON BY 133 RUNS

AUSTRALIA

M Taylor run out	26
M Slater run out	1
R Ponting c Drakes b Simmons	43
D Boon b Benjamin	4
S Waugh c Hooper b Simmons	44
G Blewett st Murray b Hooper	0
I Healy c Williams b Hooper	3
P Reiffel run out	1
S Warne b Simmons	12
D Fleming not out	5
G McGrath b Simmons	0

Sundries	10
Total 149	

Fall of Wickets: 12, 50, 59, 118, 124, 126, 127, 129, 147, 149
Bowling: C Ambrose 6-1-8-0, C Walsh 4-1-14-0,
W Benjamin 7-1-31-1, V Drakes 7-0-36-0,
C Hooper 6-0-38-2, P Simmons 4.5-0-18-4
Overs: 34.5

FOURTH LIMITED OVERS INTERNATIONAL at Arnos Vale, St Vincent
15 March 1995

AUSTRALIA

M Slater b Arthurton	68
M Taylor c Simmons b Walsh	3
M Waugh c Murray b Benjamin	26
D Boon b Arthurton	33
S Waugh c Arthurton b Simmons	25
G Blewett b Drakes	4
I Healy c Simmons b Walsh	12
P Reiffel c Murray b Walsh	9
S Warne not out	6
C McDermott run out	11
G McGrath not out	1

Sundries	12
Total 9 for 210	

Fall of Wickets: 6, 57, 130, 137, 152, 171, 190, 190, 209
Bowling: C Ambrose 8-0-22-0, C Walsh 9-0-30-3,
W Benjamin 7-0-32-1, V Drakes 7-0-36-1,
K Arthurton 10-0-45-2, P Simmons 7-0-40-1
Overs: 48
WEST INDIES WON RAIN AFFECTED GAME ON SUPERIOR RUN RATE

WEST INDIES

P Simmons c Healy b Warne	86
S Campbell st Healy b Warne	20
J Adams b McGrath	3
C Hooper not out	60
K Arthurton not out	22

Sundries	17
Total 3 for 208	

Fall of Wickets: 47, 56, 152
Bowling: C McDermott 9-1-46-0, P Reiffel 9-1-37-0,
G McGrath 10-1-40-1, S Warne 9.1-3-33-2,
G Blewett 3-0-26-0, D Boon 3-0-14-0
Overs: 43.1

FIFTH LIMITED OVERS INTERNATIONAL *at Georgetown, Guyana*
18 March 1995

AUSTRALIA

M Taylor c Adams b Hooper	66
M Slater c Holder b Drakes	41
M Waugh run out	70
S Waugh c Benjamin b Hooper	11
R Ponting b Hooper	0
J Langer run out	6
I Healy c Williams b Simmons	36
P Reiffel c Campbell b Benjamin	22
B Julian b Walsh	11
T May not out	3
Sundries	20
Total 9 for 286	

Fall of Wickets: 78, 166, 203, 203, 205, 229, 259, 276, 286
Bowling: P Simmons 10-0-54-1, C Walsh 8-2-38-1,
K Arthurton 7-0-48-0, C Hooper 10-0-36-3
W Benjamin 9-0-51-1, V Drakes 6-0-46-1,
Overs: 50
WEST INDIES WON BY 5 WICKETS
WEST INDIES WON SERIES 4-1

WEST INDIES

S Williams c and b M Waugh	45
S Campbell b Reiffel	9
P Simmons c Slater b S Waugh	70
C Hooper c Slater b Reiffel	50
J Adams not out	60
K Arthurton c M Waugh b McGrath	0
R Holder not out	34
Sundries	19
Total 5 for 287	

Fall of Wickets: 17, 108, 172, 192, 193
Bowling: P Reiffel 10-1-48-2, B Julian 10-1-66-0,
T May 7-0-42-0, G McGrath 8.2-0-51-1, M Waugh 3-0-23-1,
S Waugh 9-0-47-1
Overs: 47.2

FIRST TEST *at Kensington Oval, Barbados*
31 March, 1, 2 April 1995

WEST INDIES — FIRST INNINGS

S Williams c Taylor b Julian	1
S Campbell c Healy b Reiffel	0
B Lara c S Waugh b Julian	65
R Richardson c Healy b Julian	0
C Hooper c Taylor b Julian	60
J Adams c Warne b McGrath	16
J Murray c Taylor b McGrath	21
W Benjamin c Taylor b Warne	14
C Ambrose c Blewett b McGrath	7
C Walsh c S Waugh b Warne	1
K Benjamin not out	0
Sundries	10
Total 195	

Fall of Wickets: 1, 5, 6, 130, 152, 156, 184, 193, 194, 195
Bowling: P Reiffel 11-4-41-1, B Julian 12-0-36-4,
M Waugh 1-0-12-0, S Warne 12-2-57-2,
G McGrath 12.1-1-46-3

AUSTRALIA — FIRST INNINGS

M Slater c Williams b W Benjamin	18
M Taylor c Hooper b K Benjamin	55
D Boon c W Benjamin b Walsh	20
M Waugh c Murray b Ambrose	40
S Waugh c Murray b K Benjamin	65
G Blewett c Murray b Ambrose	14
I Healy not out	74
B Julian c K Benjamin b Hooper	31
P Reiffel b W Benjamin	1
S Warne c Adams b Walsh	6
G McGrath b W Benjamin	4
Sundries	18
Total 346	

Fall of Wickets: 27, 72, 121, 166, 194, 230, 290, 291,
331, 346
Bowling: C Ambrose 20-7-41-2, C Walsh 25-5-78-2,
K Benjamin 20-1-84-2, W Benjamin 23.2-6-71-3,
C Hooper 12-0-59-1

WEST INDIES — SECOND INNINGS

S Williams c Healy b McGrath	10
S Campbell c S Waugh b Warne	6
B Lara c Healy b McGrath	9
R Richardson b Reiffel	36
C Hooper c Reiffel b Julian	16
J Adams not out	39
J Murray c S Waugh b Warne	23
W Benjamin lbw b McGrath	26
C Ambrose c Blewett b McGrath	6
C Walsh b McGrath	4
K Benjamin b Warne	5
Sundries	9
Total	189

Fall of Wicket: 19, 25, 31, 51, 91, 136, 170, 176, 180, 189
Bowling: P Reiffel 11-6-15-1, B Julian 12-2-41-1,
S Warne 26.3-5-64-3, G McGrath 22-6-68-5
AUSTRALIA WON BY 10 WICKETS

AUSTRALIA — SECOND INNINGS

M Slater not out	20
M Taylor not out	16
Sundries	3
Total 0 for	39

Bowling: C Walsh 3-0-19-0, K Benjamin 2.5-1-14-0,
C Hooper 1-0-6-0

SECOND TEST at Recreation Ground, St John's, Antigua
8, 9, 10, 12, 13 April 1995

AUSTRALIA — FIRST INNINGS

M Slater c Adams b Walsh	41
M Taylor c Walsh b Ambrose	37
D Boon b Walsh	21
M Waugh c Hooper b Walsh	4
S Waugh b K Benjamin	15
G Blewett c Murray b W Benjamin	11
I Healy c Walsh b W Benjamin	14
B Julian b Walsh	22
P Reiffel not out	22
S Warne c Arthurton b Walsh	11
G McGrath c Murray b Walsh	0
Sundries	18
Total	216

Fall of Wickets: 82, 84, 89, 126, 126, 150, 168, 188,
204, 216
Bowling: C Ambrose 14-5-34-1, C Walsh 21.3-7-54-6,
K Benjamin 16-3-58-1, W Benjamin 15-2-40-2,
C Hooper 23-0-18-0

WEST INDIES — FIRST INNINGS

S Williams c Boon b Warne	16
R Richardson c S Waugh b Julian	37
B Lara c Boon b S Waugh	88
J Adams lbw b Warne	22
C Hooper c Julian b S Waugh	11
K Arthurton c Taylor b Warne	26
J Murray lbw b Reiffel	26
W Benjamin c Taylor b McGrath	4
C Ambrose c Taylor b Reiffel	0
C Walsh b Reiffel	9
K Benjamin not out	5
Sundries	16
Total	260

Fall of Wickets: 34, 106, 168, 186, 187, 240, 240, 240,
254, 260
Bowling: P Reiffel 17-3-53-3, B Julian 10-5-36-1,
S Warne 28-9-83-3, G McGrath 20.1-5-59-1,
S Waugh 6-1-20-2

AUSTRALIA — SECOND INNINGS

M Slater c Richardson b Walsh	18
M Taylor c Murray b Walsh	5
D Boon lbw b W Benjamin	67
M Waugh b W Benjamin	61
S Waugh not out	65
G Blewett c Williams b Hooper	19
I Healy c Hooper b Walsh	26
B Julian run out	6
P Reiffel not out	13
Sundries	20
Total 7 (dec)	300

Fall of Wickets: 22, 43, 149, 162, 196, 254, 273
Bowling: C Ambrose 19-3-42-0, C Walsh 36-7-92-3,
W Benjamin 24-2-72-2, K Benjamin 15-1-51-0,
K Arthurton 1-0-1-0, C Hooper 9-3-16-1, J Adams 4-0-16-0
MATCH DRAWN

WEST INDIES — SECOND INNINGS

S Williams not out	31
R Richardson b Reiffel	2
B Lara b Julian	43
J Adams not out	3
Sundries	1
Total 2 for	80

Fall of Wickets: 11, 69
Bowling: P Reiffel 6-2-12-1, B Julian 5-2-15-1,
S Warne 7-0-18-0, G McGrath 6-2-20-0, M Waugh 6-2-15-0

THIRD TEST at Queens Park Oval, Trinidad
21, 22, 23 April 1995

AUSTRALIA — FIRST INNINGS

M Taylor c Adams b Ambrose	2
M Slater c Murray b Walsh	0
D Boon c Richardson b Ambrose	18
M Waugh c Murray b Ambrose	2
S Waugh not out	63
G Blewett c Murray b W Benjamin	17
I Healy c Richardson b Walsh	8
B Julian c Adams b K Benjamin	0
P Reiffel c Lara b Walsh	11
S Warne b Ambrose	0
G McGrath c Murray b Ambrose	0
Sundries	7
Total	128

Fall of Wickets: 2, 2, 14, 37, 62, 95, 98, 121, 128, 128
Bowling: C Ambrose 16-5-45-5, C Walsh 17-4-50-3,
W Benjamin 6-3-13-1, K Benjamin 8-2-14-1

WEST INDIES — FIRST INNINGS

S Williams c Taylor b Reiffel	0
R Richardson c Healy b McGrath	2
B Lara c Taylor b McGrath	24
J Adams c M Waugh b Reiffel	42
C Hooper c Reiffel b S Waugh	21
K Arthurton c M Waugh b McGrath	5
J Murray c Healy b McGrath	13
W Benjamin c Slater b Warne	7
C Ambrose c Slater b McGrath	1
C Walsh c Blewett b McGrath	14
K Benjamin not out	1
Sundries	5
Total	136

Fall of Wickets: 1, 6, 42, 87, 95, 106, 113, 114, 129, 136
Bowling: G McGrath 21.5-11-47-6, P Reiffel 16-7-26-2,
B Julian 7-1-24-0, S Waugh 3-1-19-1, S Warne 12-5-16-1

AUSTRALIA — SECOND INNINGS

M Taylor c Murray b K Benjamin	30
M Slater c Richardson b Walsh	15
D Boon c (sub) Chanderpaul b Walsh	9
M Waugh lbw b Ambrose	7
S Waugh c Hooper b K Benjamin	21
G Blewett c Murray b K Benjamin	2
I Healy b Ambrose	0
B Julian b Ambrose	0
P Reiffel c Hooper b Ambrose	6
S Warne c Hooper b Walsh	11
G McGrath not out	0

Sundries	4
Total	105

Fall of Wickets: 26, 52, 56, 85, 85, 85, 87, 87, 105, 105
Bowling: C Ambrose 10.1-1-20-4, C Walsh 13-4-35-3,
W Benjamin 5-0-15-0, K Benjamin 8-1-32-3
WEST INDIES WON BY 9 WICKETS

WET INDIES — SECOND INNINGS

S Williams c Warne b M Waugh	42
R Richardson not out	38
B Lara not out	14

Sundries	4
Total 1 for	98

Fall of Wicket: 81
Bowling: G McGrath 6-1-22-0, P Reiffel 6-2-21-0,
B Julian 3-0-16-0, S Warne 3.5-0-26-0, M Waugh 2-0-9-1

FOURTH TEST at Sabina Park, Kingston, Jamaica
29, 30 April 1, 3 May 1995

WEST INDIES — FIRST INNINGS

S Williams c Blewett b Reiffel	0
R Richardson lbw b Reiffel	100
B Lara c Healy b Warne	65
J Adams c Slater b Julian	20
C Hooper c M Waugh b Julian	23
K Arthurton c Healy b McGrath	16
C Browne c Boon b Warne	1
W Benjamin lbw b S Waugh	7
C Ambrose not out	6
C Walsh c Boon b S Waugh	2
K Benjamin c Healy b Reiffel	5

Sundries	20
Total	265

Fall of Wickets: 0, 103, 131, 188, 220, 243, 250, 251, 254, 265
Bowling: P Reiffel 13.4-2-48-3, G McGrath 20-4-79-1,
S Warne 25-6-72-2, S Waugh 11-5-14-2, M Waugh 4-1-11-0,
B Julian 12-3-31-2

AUSTRALIA — FIRST INNINGS

M Taylor c Adams b Walsh	8
M Slater c Lara b Walsh	27
D Boon c Browne b Ambrose	17
M Waugh c Adams b Hooper	126
S Waugh c Lara b K Benjamin	200
G Blewett c W Benjamin b Arthurton	69
I Healy c Lara b W Benjamin	6
B Julian c Adams b Walsh	8
P Reiffel b K Benjamin	23
S Warne c Lara b K Benjamin	0
G McGrath not out	3

Sundries	44
Total	531

Fall of Wickets: 17, 50, 73, 304, 417, 433, 449, 522, 522, 531
Bowling: C Ambrose 21-4-76-1, C Walsh 33-6-103-3,
K Benjamin 23.5-0-106-3, W Benjamin 24-3-80-1,
C Hooper 43-9-94-1, J Adams, 11-0-38-0
K Arthurton 5-1-17-1

WEST INDIES — SECOND INNINGS

S Williams b Reiffel	20
R Richardson c and b Reiffel	14
B Lara lbw b Reiffel	0
J Adams c S Waugh b McGrath	18
W Benjamin lbw b Reiffel	51
C Hooper run out	13
K Arthurton lbw b Warne	14
C Browne not out	31
C Ambrose st Healy b Warne	5
C Walsh c Blewett b Warne	14
K Benjamin c Taylor b Warne	6
Sundries	27
	Total 213

Fall of Wickets: 37, 37, 46, 98, 134, 140, 166, 172, 204, 213
Bowling: P Reiffel 18-5-47-4, B Julian 10-2-37-0,
S Warne 23.4-8-70-4, M Waugh 1-0-1-0,
G McGrath 13-2-28-1, S Waugh 4-0-9-0
AUSTRALIA WON BY AN INNINGS AND 53 RUNS
AUSTRALIA WON TEST SERIES 2-1

Australia -v- West Indies
Test Averages

AUSTRALIAN TEST BATTING AVERAGES

	M	Inn	N.O.	Runs	H.S.	Avrge	Ct	St
Steve Waugh	4	6	2	429	200	107.25	6	-
Mark Waugh	4	6	-	240	126	40.00	3	-
Ian Healy	4	6	1	128	74*	25.60	10	1
Mark Taylor	4	7	1	153	55	25.50	9	-
David Boon	4	6	-	152	67	25.33	4	-
Michael Slater	4	7	1	139	41	23.17	3	-
Greg Blewett	4	6	-	132	69	22.00	5	-
Paul Reiffel	4	6	2	76	23	19.00	3	-
Brendon Julian	4	6	-	67	31	11.17	1	-
Shane Warne	4	5	-	28	11	5.60	2	-
Glenn McGrath	4	5	2	7	4	2.33	-	-

AUSTRALIAN TEST BOWLING AVERAGES

	M	Overs	Mdns	Runs	Wkts	Avrge	Best
Steve Waugh	4	24.0	7	62	5	12.40	2/14
Paul Reiffel	4	98.4	31	263	15	17.53	4/47
Glenn McGrath	4	121.1	32	369	17	21.71	6/47
Brendon Julian	4	71.0	15	236	9	26.22	4/36
Shane Warne	4	138.0	35	406	15	27.07	4/70
Mark Waugh	4	14.0	3	48	1	48.00	1/9

WEST INDIES TEST BATTING AVERAGES

	M	Inn	N.O.	Runs	H.S.	Avrge	Ct	St
Brian Lara	4	8	1	308	88	44.00	5	-
Richie Richardson	4	8	1	229	100	32.71	4	-
Jimmy Adams	4	7	2	160	42	32.00	7	-
Courtney Browne	1	2	1	32	31*	32.00	1	-
Carl Hooper	4	6	-	144	60	24.00	6	-
Junior Murray	3	4	-	83	26	20.75	12	-
Winston Benjamin	4	6	-	109	51	18.17	2	-
Stuart Williams	4	8	1	120	42	17.14	2	-
Keith Arthurton	3	4	-	61	26	15.25	1	-
Courtney Walsh	4	6	-	44	14	7.33	2	-
Kenny Benjamin	4	6	3	22	6	7.33	1	-
Curtly Ambrose	4	6	1	25	7	5.00	-	-
Sherwin Campbell	1	2	-	6	6	3.00	-	-

WEST INDIES TEST BOWLING AVERAGES

	M	Overs	Mdns	Runs	Wkts	Avrge	Best
Keith Arthurton	3	6.0	1	18	1	18.00	1/17
Curtly Ambrose	4	100.1	25	258	13	19.85	5/45
Courtney Walsh	4	148.3	33	431	20	21.55	6/54
Winston Benjamin	4	97.2	16	291	9	32.33	3/71
Kenny Benjamin	4	93.4	9	359	10	35.90	3/32
Carl Hooper	4	67.0	12	193	3	64.33	1/16
Jimmy Adams	4	15.0	-	54	-	-	-

NSW Father of the Year, 1995

The prize that probably meant most of all to Mark Taylor in his crowded year-and-a-bit had nothing to do with cricket. Or very little anyway. In late August at a luncheon at the Menzies Hotel, downtown Sydney, Taylor was named NSW Father of the Year.

'Because of the nature of my life in cricket I have to do my best to be a quality father, not a quantity father', Taylor told the assembled gathering in a warm and often touching speech. Australia's captain told how the look in son William's eye when Mark had climbed into a taxi outside home, bound for Mascot and then to the West Indies, had been the most painful, difficult event of the whole tour for him. The other side of the coin was the reunion at the airport with William, baby Jack and wife Judi. William endured manfully for a while the obligatory press conference that his father had to work his way through. Eventually it became too much and William climbed off his chair in the room and took a place on his father's knee at the conference table. 'Dad, can we go now?' he whispered.

Mark's being named Father of the Year was a beautiful coincidence. Mark Taylor, on August 25, became the 39th winner of the award. As has been noted earlier in these pages, he is also Australia's 39th cricket captain. He joined two

William, Jack, Judi and Mark Taylor at the NSW Father of the Year luncheon.

other notable sportsmen in winning the award — yachting's Sir James Hardy, and the great all-rounder and former tennis player, Alan Davidson, AM, MBE, who — as president of the NSW Cricket Association — has been a prominent figure in Mark's own cricketing life.

Outside it was very much cricket weather. An early spring had arrived after the long, dry winter and the weather gave its own hint of a hard, hot summer of cricket ahead. For the 200 guests, Mark's speech drove home the sacrifices made by top sports people — the loss of family time endured, especially in the game of cricket with its long, unfolding tours.

Now it was all about to start again. Another summer, another season of cricket. Weeks in hotel rooms around Australia, far from home. Lonely times. As Mark observed, that just happens to be the nature of the job. But today everyone was together. Today Australia's captain was a happy and proud father. He was about to become a cricketer again. But tomorrow would do for that . . .